THE ULTIMATE

BEER COOKBOOK

121 HILARIOUS AND EASY RECIPES TO IMPRESS FAMILY AND FRIENDS.

SUITABLE FOR BEGINNERS

BY LUCAS WILSON

Table Of Contents

Table Of Contents

Table Of Contents

Table Of Contents

Debra's Pickled Eggs in Beer

Ingredients

24 small hard-cooked eggs
1 (12 fluid ounce) bottle beer
2 cups vinegar
1 tablespoon pickling spice
1 tablespoon parsley flakes

Directions

Place eggs in a large stock pot and cover with cold water. You may need to cook the eggs in 2 batches if you do not have a pot large enough. Bring to a boil and immediately remove from heat. Cover, and let stand in hot water for 10 to 12 minutes. Cool under cold running water, and peel. Pierce each egg with a knife or fork to assist in the absorption of liquid.

Transfer eggs to a large glass jar or other deep, sealable glass container. Place beer, vinegar, pickling spice, and parsley flakes together in a bowl. Pour over eggs until fully submerged. (Be sure to select a container in which the eggs are completely covered, or add additional pickling liquid, if necessary.) Cover and refrigerate for at least 3 days before using. Can be sealed and stored in the refrigerator for up to 2 weeks in pickling liquid.

Dizzy Pineapple Bread

Ingredients

(8 ounce) can pineapple chunks
3/4 cups self-rising flour
/3 cup white sugar
(12 fluid ounce) can or bottle
eer

Directions

Preheat oven to 350 degrees F (175 degrees C). Grease one 9x5 inch baking pan.

Combine the pineapple flour, sugar and beer. Do not overmix! Pour batter into the prepared pan.

Bake at 350 degrees F (175 degrees C) for about 1 hour or until bread tests done.

Slow Cooker Pork Tenderloin with Beer and

Ingredients

1 (2 pound) pork tenderloin
6 fluid ounces lager-style beer (such as Molson Canadian ®)
2 tablespoons white wine vinegar
2 potatoes, quartered
2 carrots, quartered
6 button mushrooms
2 cloves garlic
1/2 small onion, cut into chunks
1 1/2 teaspoons salt
1 teaspoon whole black peppercorns
1 teaspoon dried sage

Directions

Combine the pork tenderloin, beer, vinegar, potatoes, carrots, mushrooms, garlic, onion, salt, peppercorns, and sage in a slow cooker. Cover and cook on low for 4 hours.

Nova Scotia Beer Warmer

Ingredients

(12 fluid ounce) can beer
 dashes hot pepper sauce (e.g.
abascoв„ў)

Directions

Pour the beer into a mug or tall glass, and add a few dashes of hot sauce. Drink.

Beer Batter Crepes I

Ingredients

3 eggs, lightly beaten
1 cup milk
1 cup beer
1 3/4 cups all-purpose flour
1 pinch salt
2 tablespoons vegetable oil
2 tablespoons butter

Directions

In a large bowl, whisk together eggs, milk and beer. Gradually whisk in flour. Add the salt and oil, then whisk the batter vigorously for 3 to 5 minutes, so all is thoroughly incorporated. Let the batter sit for 1 hour.

Heat a 10 inch non-stick skillet over medium heat. Brush it with butter, and when it's hot but not smoking, pour a scant 1/3 cup of batter into the center of the skillet, and rotate it so the batter covers the bottom of the pan in a thin layer, pouring out any excess batter. Cook the crepe until it is just golden on one side, 1 to 2 minutes, turn it and cook until it is golden on the other side, about 30 seconds. Transfer to a plate, and keep warm by covering with aluminum foil. Continue until all of the batter is used.

Slow Cooked Corned Beef for Sandwiches

ngredients

: (3 pound) corned beef briskets
vith spice packets
: (12 fluid ounce) bottles beer
: bay leaves
/4 cup peppercorns
 bulb garlic cloves, separated
ind peeled

Directions

Place the corned beef briskets into a large pot. Sprinkle in one of the spice packets, and discard the other one or save for other uses. Pour in the beer, and fill the pot with enough water to cover the briskets by 1 inch. Add the bay leaves, peppercorns and garlic cloves. Cover, and bring to a boil.

Once the liquid comes to a boil, reduce the heat to medium-low, and simmer for 4 to 5 hours, checking hourly, and adding more water if necessary to keep the meat covered.

Carefully remove the meat from the pot, as it will be extremely tender. Set on a cutting board, and allow it to rest until it firms up a bit, about 10 minutes. Slice or shred to serve. I discard the cooking liquid, but it can be used to cook cabbage and other vegetables if desired.

Beef and Irish Stout Stew

Ingredients

2 pounds lean beef stew meat, cut into 1-inch cubes
3 tablespoons vegetable oil, divided
2 tablespoons all-purpose flour
1 pinch salt and ground black pepper to taste
1 pinch cayenne pepper
2 large onions, chopped
1 clove garlic, crushed
2 tablespoons tomato paste
1 1/2 cups Irish stout beer (such as Guinness®)
2 cups chopped carrot
1 sprig fresh thyme
1 tablespoon chopped fresh parsley for garnish

Directions

Toss the beef cubes with 1 tablespoon of vegetable oil. In a separate bowl, stir together the flour, salt, pepper, and cayenne pepper. Dredge the beef in this to coat.

Heat the remaining oil in a deep skillet or Dutch oven over medium-high heat. Add the beef, and brown on all sides. Add the onions, and garlic. Stir the tomato paste into a small amount of water to dilute; pour into the pan and stir to blend. Reduce the heat to medium, cover, and cook for 5 minutes.

Pour 1/2 cup of the beer into the pan, and as it begins to boil, scrape any bits of food from the bottom of the pan with a wooden spoon. This adds a lot of flavor to the broth. Pour in the rest of the beer, and add the carrots and thyme. Cover, reduce heat to low, and simmer for 2 to 3 hours, stirring occasionally. Taste and adjust seasoning before serving. Garnish with chopped parsley.

Margie's Cuban Sofrito (Sauce)

Ingredients

tablespoons vegetable oil
medium onion, chopped
green bell pepper, seeded and chopped
cloves garlic, chopped
teaspoon salt
/4 teaspoon pepper
/4 teaspoon ground cumin
teaspoon dried oregano, crushed
bay leaves
tomatoes, chopped (optional)
/4 cup canned tomato sauce

Directions

Heat oil in a skillet over medium-high heat. Add onion and garlic, and cook until onion is translucent. Add the bell pepper, and saute until tender. Season with salt, pepper, cumin, oregano and bay leaves. Continue cooking until the mixture looks like a yummy green paste with oil around it. Stir in the tomatoes, if using, and cook stirring until all of the liquid is released. Gradually stir in the tomato sauce simmer until the sauce looks really red. Taste, and adjust seasonings if desired. Remove bay leaves.

Now the sauce is done. You can add it to meat, rice, beans fish or potatoes. Thin the sauce down if necessary with water, wine, beer, or whatever is handy.

Harvest Beef Stew

Ingredients

4 tablespoons bacon drippings
1/4 cup flour
Salt and pepper to taste
2 1/2 pounds beef stew meat, cut into 1 inch cubes
5 tablespoons olive oil
1 onion, thinly sliced
6 cloves garlic, thinly sliced
1 pound carrots, peeled and sliced
1 pound celery, sliced
1/4 cup rice vinegar
2 tablespoons brown sugar
4 cups beef broth
2 (12 fluid ounce) cans or bottles ale
1 parsnip, peeled and sliced
1 turnip, peeled and chopped
1 pound baby red potatoes, washed
3/4 cup parsley, chopped
4 whole bay leaves

Directions

Heat bacon grease in a large pot over medium heat.

Combine flour with salt and pepper. Coat beef cubes.

Brown meat in the bacon grease until nicely browned. Remove to a paper towel, and set aside.

Heat olive oil in the same pot. Cook onions, garlic, carrots, and celery over low heat. Add the vinegar and sugar. Pour in the broth and bring to a boil. Deglaze the pan by scraping off the food stuck on the bottom of the pot.

Return meat to pot. Pour in beer, then stir in parsnips, turnips, red potatoes, parsley, and bay leaves. Reduce heat to medium low. Cover and simmer for 90 minutes, stirring occasionally.

Chad's Slow Cooker Taco Soup

Ingredients

pound ground beef
pound bulk hot pork sausage
(28 ounce) can crushed
omatoes
(15.25 ounce) can whole kernel
orn with red and green bell
eppers (such as Mexicorn®),
rained and rinsed
(14.5 ounce) can black beans,
insed and drained
(14 ounce) can kidney beans,
insed and drained
(1 ounce) package ranch
ressing mix
(1 ounce) package taco
easoning mix
onion, chopped
green bell pepper, chopped
red bell pepper, chopped
(14.5 ounce) can diced tomatoes
with green chile peppers (such as
RO*TEL®), undrained
/2 cup chili sauce
fresh jalapeno peppers, diced
(12 fluid ounce) can or bottle
ark beer
round black pepper to taste

Directions

Brown the ground beef completely in a large skillet over medium heat; drain. Transfer the beef to a slow cooker.

Brown the sausage completely in a large skillet over medium heat; drain. Transfer the beef to a slow cooker.

Add the crushed tomatoes, corn, black beans, kidney beans, ranch dressing mix, taco seasoning mix, onion, green bell pepper, red bell pepper, diced tomatoes with green chile peppers, chili sauce, jalapeno peppers, beer, and black pepper to the slow cooker. Set slow cooker to Low and cook 8 to 10 hours, or, if you prefer, on High for 4 to 6 hours.

Chicken Fajita Marinade

Ingredients

1/4 cup beer
1/3 cup fresh lime juice
1 tablespoon olive oil
2 cloves garlic, minced
1 tablespoon brown sugar
1 tablespoon Worcestershire sauce
1 tablespoon chopped cilantro
1/2 teaspoon ground cumin
salt to taste

Directions

To prepare the marinade, stir together beer, lime juice, olive oil, garlic, brown sugar, Worcestershire sauce, cilantro, cumin, and salt; mix well.

To use marinade, pour into a resealable plastic bag, add up to 1 1/2 pounds of chicken breast, and mix until chicken is well coated. Marinate for 1 to 3 hours in the refrigerator.

Ingredients

(12 fluid ounce) can frozen
meade concentrate
2 fluid ounces tequila
2 fluid ounces water
2 fluid ounces beer
e
lime, cut into wedges

Directions

Pour limeade, tequila, water, and beer into a large pitcher. Stir until well-blended, and limeade has melted. Add plenty of ice, and garnish with lime wedges. Adjust with additional water, if needed.

Beer Roasted Lime Chicken

Ingredients

1 (4 pound) whole chicken
1 tablespoon salt, or to taste
1 tablespoon ground black pepper, or to taste
1 lime, halved
1/2 (12 fluid ounce) can beer
1 cup water

Directions

Preheat the oven to 350 degrees F (175 degrees C).

Season the chicken inside and out with salt and pepper. Squeeze the juice from the lime over the whole chicken, then place the halves into the cavity of the chicken. Set the half full beer can in the center of a roasting pan or baking dish, and place the chicken over it in an upright position with the beer inserted into the cavity. Pour water into the bottom of the pan. Cover the chicken with aluminum foil, and place roasting pan and all into the oven.

Roast the chicken for about 1 1/2 hours in the preheated oven, removing foil during the last 20 minutes. Baste occasionally with the drippings. When finished, the internal temperature of the chicken should be 180 degrees F (80 degrees C) when taken in the meatiest part of the thigh. Let the chicken rest for about 10 minutes before serving.

Drunken Dogs

Ingredients

(16 ounce) packages beef
frankfurters, cut into bite size
pieces

cup light brown sugar

(12 fluid ounce) can or bottle
beer

Directions

In a medium saucepan, place the frankfurters, brown sugar and beer. Bring to boil. Reduce heat and simmer at least 1 hour.

Boilermaker Tailgate Chili

Ingredients

2 pounds ground beef chuck
1 pound bulk Italian sausage
3 (15 ounce) cans chili beans, drained
1 (15 ounce) can chili beans in spicy sauce
2 (28 ounce) cans diced tomatoes with juice
1 (6 ounce) can tomato paste
1 large yellow onion, chopped
3 stalks celery, chopped
1 green bell pepper, seeded and chopped
1 red bell pepper, seeded and chopped
2 green chile peppers, seeded and chopped
1 tablespoon bacon bits
4 cubes beef bouillon
1/2 cup beer
1/4 cup chili powder
1 tablespoon Worcestershire sauce
1 tablespoon minced garlic
1 tablespoon dried oregano
2 teaspoons ground cumin
2 teaspoons hot pepper sauce (e. g. Tabascoв„ÿ)
1 teaspoon dried basil
1 teaspoon salt
1 teaspoon ground black pepper
1 teaspoon cayenne pepper
1 teaspoon paprika
1 teaspoon white sugar
1 (10.5 ounce) bag corn chips such as FritosB®
1 (8 ounce) package shredded Cheddar cheese

Directions

Heat a large stock pot over medium-high heat. Crumble the ground chuck and sausage into the hot pan, and cook until evenly browned. Drain off excess grease.

Pour in the chili beans, spicy chili beans, diced tomatoes and tomato paste. Add the onion, celery, green and red bell peppers, chile peppers, bacon bits, bouillon, and beer. Season with chili powder, Worcestershire sauce, garlic, oregano, cumin, hot pepper sauce, basil, salt, pepper, cayenne, paprika, and sugar. Stir to blend, then cover and simmer over low heat for at least 2 hours, stirring occasionally.

After 2 hours, taste, and adjust salt, pepper, and chili powder if necessary. The longer the chili simmers, the better it will taste. Remove from heat and serve, or refrigerate, and serve the next day.

To serve, ladle into bowls, and top with corn chips and shredded Cheddar cheese.

Grilled Jamaican Jerked Pork Loin Chops

ngredients

/2 (12 ounce) bottle lager style
eer
 fluid ounces dark rum
/4 cup molasses
/4 cup soy sauce
/4 cup lime juice
 tablespoons minced garlic
 tablespoons minced ginger
 scotch bonnet chile pepper,
inced
 teaspoons chopped fresh thyme
 teaspoons chopped fresh
arjoram
 1/2 teaspoons ground allspice
 teaspoons ground cinnamon
 teaspoon ground nutmeg
 bay leaves

 (6 ounce) pork loin chops
osher salt and cracked black
epper to taste

Directions

Pour the beer, rum, molasses, soy sauce, and lime juice into a bowl.
Stir in the garlic, ginger, scotch bonnet pepper, thyme, and
marjoram. Season with allspice, cinnamon, nutmeg, and bay
leaves. Place the pork chops into a zip top bag, and pour in the
marinade. Refrigerate overnight.

Prepare an outdoor grill for medium heat. Take the pork chops out
of the marinade, place on a plate, and allow to sit at room
temperature for 15 to 20 minutes as the grill heats.

Season the chops to taste with kosher salt and cracked black
pepper. Grill the chops on both sides until a thermometer inserted
into the center registers 150 degrees F. Allow the pork chops to
rest for about 5 minutes before serving to allow the juices to
redistribute.

Flaming Doctor Pepper II

Ingredients

2 fluid ounces amaretto liqueur
1/2 fluid ounce 151 proof rum
1 (1.5 fluid ounce) jigger beer

Directions

Pour amaretto into a highball glass. Gently pour the rum over the back of a spoon, so that it forms a layer on top of the amaretto. Carefully light rum with a match. Pour in the beer, wait for flames to die down, and drink entire contents in one gulp.

ngredients

(20 ounce) loaf round French
read
 (8 ounce) packages cream
heese, softened
 tablespoons grated onion
 tablespoons beer
 teaspoons Worcestershire sauce
 teaspoons lemon juice
 teaspoon hot pepper sauce
/2 teaspoon salt
 (6.5 ounce) cans minced clams,
rained

Directions

Preheat oven to 250 degrees F (120 degrees C).

Cut off top of bread and set aside. Hollow loaf, leaving 1 1/2 to 2 inch shell. Reserve the bread that you pull out of the loaf.

In a medium-size bowl, combine cream cheese, onion, beer, Worcestershire sauce, lemon juice, hot pepper sauce, and salt. Beat well. Fold clams into the mixture. Pour clam mixture into the hollowed out bread bowl, cover the bread bowl with the bread top. Wrap the loaf in aluminum foil.

Bake at 250 degrees F (120 degrees C) for 3 hours. Use the leftover bread torn from inside the loaf to make bread cubes to dip with. Toast bread cubes with dip during last 5 minutes of baking time.

Best Beer Cheese Soup

Ingredients

5 slices bacon
2 tablespoons butter or margarine
1 onion, diced
1 carrot, diced
1 celery rib, diced
1 teaspoon dried basil
1 teaspoon dried oregano
1 bunch green onions, chopped
2 tablespoons flour
2 cups chicken broth
2 (12 fluid ounce) cans or bottles domestic beer
1 pound processed cheese food, cubed
1/2 pound sharp Cheddar cheese, grated
2 teaspoons garlic powder

Directions

Place bacon in a large, deep skillet. Cook over medium-high heat until evenly brown; drain on plate lined with paper towels; crumble.

Melt the butter in a skillet over medium heat. Cook the onion, carrot, and celery in the butter until soft, 7 to 10 minutes. Add the bacon, basil, oregano, and green onions; cook and stir 2 minutes. Stir the flour into the mixture until completely dissolved. Pour in the chicken broth and beer; cook until heated through. Melt the processed cheese food and Cheddar cheese in the mixture in small batches. Season with garlic powder and stir.

ngredients

pound ground beef
small onion, finely chopped
cloves garlic, minced
 tablespoon Worcestershire
auce
 teaspoon salt
/4 teaspoon ground black
epper
/4 cup beer

Directions

Preheat an outdoor grill for medium-high heat and lightly oil the grate.

Mix the ground beef, onion, garlic, Worcestershire sauce, salt, and pepper in a bowl. Mix in the beer until absorbed by the meat mixture. Form into patties.

Cook on the preheated grill until the burgers are cooked to your desired degree of doneness, about 5 minutes per side for well done. An instant-read thermometer inserted into the center should read 160 degrees F (70 degrees C).

Ingredients

4 cups bread flour
2 tablespoons honey
1/4 teaspoon salt
1 tablespoon margarine
10 ounces dark beer
1 (.25 ounce) package active dry yeast
1 pinch ground cinnamon
2 tablespoons butter, melted

Directions

Allow 10 to 12 ounces of beer to reach room temperature and go flat. This will take approximately 3 to 4 hours.

Combine flattened beer, butter, cinnamon, salt, and honey in the pan of bread machine. Add flour and yeast being careful that the yeast does not touch the liquid. Select Dough setting, and Start.

After the dough has risen, remove the dough from the pan. Form into a long loaf; cut and form rolls. Place on a floured baking sheet, cover, and allow to rise for approximately 45 minutes.

Brush top of rolls with melted butter.

Bake at 350 degrees F (175 degrees C) for 30 minutes, or until golden brown.

Ingredients

/2 cup chopped green onions
cup sliced celery
cup sliced carrots
ounces fresh mushrooms, sliced
/4 cup butter
/2 cup all-purpose flour
teaspoon mustard powder
cups chicken broth
small head cauliflower
(12 fluid ounce) can or bottle
beer
ounces sharp Cheddar cheese,
shredded
tablespoons grated Parmesan
cheese
salt to taste
ground black pepper to taste

Directions

Saute green onions, celery, carrots, and mushrooms in butter. Mix flour and dry mustard into sauteed vegetables. Add chicken broth, bring to a boil.

Break up cauliflower into bite-size pieces, steam until just tender.

Reduce heat of sauteed vegetables to a simmer, add cauliflower, beer, and cheeses. Simmer 15-20 minutes. Add salt and pepper to taste. Check seasonings.

New Orleans Shrimp

Ingredients

1 teaspoon canola oil
1 onion, finely diced
1 stalk celery, chopped
1 green bell pepper, chopped
1 teaspoon crushed red pepper
1 tablespoon butter
1/4 cup all-purpose flour
1/2 teaspoon salt
cracked black pepper to taste
2 1/2 cups fish stock
1 cup beer
1 pound large shrimp - peeled and deveined

Directions

Pour oil into a large, heavy skillet; place over medium high heat. Heat oil until hot, but not smoking. Reduce heat to low, and add onion, celery, and green pepper. If using diced hot peppers, stir in now. Saute until the onion is soft; be careful not to burn onion. Remove vegetables from skillet, and wipe out excess liquid with paper towel.

Return pan to heat. Melt butter in pan: let bubble, but do not allow butter to burn. Sprinkle flour over butter, and stir with wire whisk. Whisk in salt and black pepper. Whisking constantly, brown flour mixture until dry; this should take about 3 to 5 minutes. Do not allow roux to burn.

Slowly whisk in hot fish stock . Increase heat slightly. Gradually whisk in beer; keep whisking until gravy thickens. Stir in vegetables. If gravy is too thick, gradually stir in warm water to dilute.

Stir shrimp into gravy. Cook until pink, about 2 to 3 minutes. Remove from heat, and serve.

Drunken Roasted Salsa

ngredients

/2 green bell pepper
/2 red bell pepper
 fresh jalapeno peppers
 serrano peppers
 tablespoons olive oil
/4 large white onion, cut into
arge chunks
/2 large fresh tomato, chopped
 cloves garlic
/4 cup cilantro leaves
 (12 ounce) can canned diced
>matoes with their juice
 tablespoons fresh lime juice
/2 teaspoon salt
/2 teaspoon ground black
epper
 fluid ounces Mexican beer

Directions

Preheat oven to broil. Line a baking sheet with foil.

Halve the green bell pepper, red bell pepper, jalapeno peppers, and serrano peppers lengthwise and discard stems and seeds. Place on baking sheet and brush the peppers with olive oil. Roast peppers under the broiler until the skin blackens and blisters, 3 to 5 minutes. Place peppers in a bowl and cover with plastic wrap; allow the peppers to steam until the skins loosen, about 10 minutes. Peel skin off the peppers and discard.

Combine the green bell pepper, red bell pepper, jalapenos, serrano, onion, tomato, garlic, cilantro, diced tomato with juice, lime juice, salt, black pepper, and beer in a blender. Blend to desired consistency. Transfer to a bowl and allow to cool in the refrigerator for 30 minutes before serving.

Guinness® and Chocolate Cheesecake

Ingredients

1 cup crushed chocolate cookies
1/4 cup butter, softened
2 tablespoons white sugar
1/4 teaspoon unsweetened cocoa powder

3 (8 ounce) packages cream cheese, softened
1 cup white sugar
3 eggs
1/2 pound semisweet chocolate chips
2 tablespoons heavy cream
1 cup sour cream
1 pinch salt
3/4 cup Irish stout beer (e.g. Guinness®)
2 teaspoons vanilla extract

1 (1 ounce) square semisweet chocolate

Directions

Preheat oven to 350 degrees F (175 degrees C). Prepare a 9 inch springform pan with butter.

Combine the crushed cookies, butter, 2 tablespoons sugar, and cocoa in a small bowl; mix; press into the bottom of the prepared springform pan.

Place the cream cheese in a large bowl and beat with an electric mixer set to low speed until smooth. While beating, slowly add 1 cup sugar and then the eggs, one at a time. Continue beating until smooth.

Combine the chocolate chips and heavy cream in a microwave-safe bowl. Heat in the microwave until the chocolate is completely melted, stirring every 30 seconds. Beat the chocolate into the cream cheese mixture. Add the sour cream, salt, beer, and vanilla; blend until smooth. Pour the mixture over the crust. Place the pan into a large, deep baking dish. Fill the dish with water to cover the bottom half of the springform pan.

Bake the cheesecake in the water bath in the preheated oven for 45 minutes; turn oven off; leave the cheesecake in the oven with oven door slightly ajar another 45 minutes; remove from oven. Run a knife along the edge of the cheesecake to loosen from pan. Chill in refrigerator at least 4 hours.

Melt the semisweet chocolate in a small bowl using the microwave. Make chocolate clovers by dropping 3 small drops of melted chocolate close to one another on waxed paper. Drag a toothpick from between two dots outward to make the stem; chill until hardened. Arrange the chocolate clovers on top of the chilled cheesecake for decoration.

Triple Dipped Fried Chicken

Ingredients

cups all-purpose flour
1/2 tablespoons garlic salt
tablespoon ground black pepper
tablespoon paprika
/2 teaspoon poultry seasoning

1/3 cups all-purpose flour
teaspoon salt
/4 teaspoon ground black
pepper
egg yolks, beaten
1/2 cups beer or water

quart vegetable oil for frying
(3 pound) whole chicken, cut
nto pieces

Directions

In one medium bowl, mix together 3 cups of flour, garlic salt, 1 tablespoon black pepper, paprika and poultry seasoning. In a separate bowl, stir together 1 1/3 cups flour, salt, 1/4 teaspoon pepper, egg yolks and beer. You may need to thin with additional beer if the batter is too thick.

Heat the oil in a deep-fryer to 350 degrees F (175 degrees C). Moisten each piece of chicken with a little water, then dip in the dry mix. Shake off excess and dip in the wet mix, then dip in the dry mix once more.

Carefully place the chicken pieces in the hot oil. Fry for 15 to 18 minutes, or until well browned. Smaller pieces will not take as long. Large pieces may take longer. Remove and drain on paper towels before serving.

Marty's Loosemeat Sandwich

Ingredients

1 pound lean ground beef
1 (12 fluid ounce) can or bottle beer
1 teaspoon salt
1 teaspoon granulated sugar
1/2 teaspoon ground black pepper
2 teaspoons yellow mustard

Directions

In a medium skillet over medium heat, cook the ground beef until evenly browned; drain.

Stir in beer, salt, sugar, pepper, and yellow mustard. Bring to a boil, and reduce heat to low; simmer partially covered. Remove from heat the moment all the liquid has evaporated.

Corey's Brown Snapper

Ingredients

fluid ounce amaretto liqueur
fluid ounces Canadian whiskey
ice cubes
/4 cup chilled root beer

Directions

Pour the amaretto and whiskey into a glass with ice. Top with root beer. Stir and enjoy!

Beer Chicken

Ingredients

2 pounds chicken drumsticks
2 (12 fluid ounce) cans
Budweiserв„ў beer
1 teaspoon dried rosemary

Directions

Preheat the oven to 350 degrees F (175 degrees C).

Place the chicken drumsticks in a 9x13 baking dish. Season with rosemary, salt and pepper. Pour the beers in with the chicken.

Bake for 1 hour in the preheated oven, until the chicken is browned and meat slides off the bone easily. Just you wait! You are going to love it!

Beer Soup (Biersuppe)

Ingredients

cups beer

egg yolks

cup sour cream

teaspoon cornstarch

teaspoon white sugar

/2 teaspoon salt

slices French bread, cut into 1

ch cubes

cup shredded Swiss cheese

Directions

In a medium saucepan over medium heat, bring beer, covered, to a boil.

Meanwhile, in a bowl, beat together egg yolks, sour cream, cornstarch, sugar and salt until well blended. Transfer mixture to a large saucepan over low heat. Pour in hot beer, a little at a time, stirring until well combined. Do not boil.

To serve, divide bread cubes into four warmed soup bowls. Sprinkle cheese over bread. Pour hot soup over all and serve piping hot.

Monaco

Ingredients

4 fluid ounces amber beer
2 fluid ounces lemon-lime flavored carbonated beverage
1/4 teaspoon grenadine syrup

Directions

Pour the beer, soda, and grenadine syrup in a tall glass. Stir and serve.

Wisconsin Native's Beer Cheese Soup

ngredients

1/2 cups diced carrots
1/2 cups diced onion
1/2 cups diced celery
cloves garlic, minced
 teaspoon hot pepper sauce
/8 teaspoon cayenne pepper
/2 teaspoon salt
/4 teaspoon black pepper
cups chicken broth
cups beer
/3 cup butter
/3 cup flour
cups milk or half and half
 cups shredded sharp Cheddar
heese
tablespoon Dijon mustard
teaspoons Worcestershire sauce
teaspoon dry mustard
opped popcorn, for garnish

Directions

In a large saucepan over medium heat, stir together carrots, onion, celery, and garlic. Stir in hot pepper sauce, cayenne pepper, salt, and pepper. Pour in chicken broth and beer; simmer until vegetables are tender, about 12 minutes. Remove from heat.

Meanwhile, heat butter in a large soup pot over medium-high heat. Stir in flour with a wire whisk; cook, stirring until the flour is light brown, about 3 or 4 minutes. Gradually stir in milk, whisking to prevent scorching, until thickened. Remove from heat, and gradually stir in cheese. Keep warm.

Stir beer mixture into cheese mixture. Stir in Dijon mustard, Worcestershire sauce, and dry mustard. Adjust for hot pepper sauce. Bring to a simmer, and cook 10 minutes. Serve topped with popcorn.

Beer and Brown Sugar Steak Marinade

Ingredients

2 (16 ounce) beef sirloin steaks
1/4 cup dark beer
2 tablespoons teriyaki sauce
2 tablespoons brown sugar
1/2 teaspoon seasoned salt
1/2 teaspoon black pepper
1/2 teaspoon garlic powder

Directions

Preheat grill for high heat.

Use a fork to poke holes all over the surface of the steaks, and place steaks in a large baking dish. In a bowl, mix together beer, teriyaki sauce, and brown sugar. Pour sauce over steaks, and let sit about 5 minutes. Sprinkle with 1/2 the seasoned salt, pepper, and garlic powder; set aside for 10 minutes. Turn steaks over, sprinkle with remaining seasoned salt, pepper, and garlic powder, and continue marinating for 10 more minutes.

Remove steaks from marinade. Pour marinade into a small saucepan, bring to a boil, and cook for several minutes.

Lightly oil the grill grate. Grill steaks for 7 minutes per side, or to desired doneness. During the last few minutes of grilling, baste steaks with boiled marinade to enhance the flavor and ensure juiciness.

ngredients

- (1/2 pound) steaks
- (12 fluid ounce) can or bottle tout beer
- clove crushed garlic
- /4 cup soy sauce
- (10.5 ounce) can condensed eef broth
- /2 teaspoon dried sage
- teaspoon onion powder
- teaspoon freshly ground black epper

Directions

Place steaks in a flat glass dish. Use a big enough dish so that steaks lay flat on the bottom. Toss in your garlic and spices. Pour the bottle of stout, soy sauce, and beef broth over the steaks. Add just enough water to cover the steaks. Cover, and let marinate in the refrigerator overnight (or at least three hours).

Preheat the oven to broil. Cook steaks to desired doneness.

Bloody Mary Deluxe

Ingredients

1 (11.5 fl oz) can spicy vegetable juice cocktail
1/2 lime, juiced
1 stalk celery
4 dashes pepper sauce (such as Frank's Red HotB®)
2 dashes Worcestershire sauce
1 teaspoon prepared horseradish
4 (1.5 fluid ounce) jiggers vodka, or to taste
1/2 cup crushed ice
salt and ground black pepper to taste
B
1 cup ice cubes
4 marinated cocktail onions
1/2 carrot (optional)
2 short stalks of celery with leaves
2 stuffed green olives
1/2 lime, cut into wedges
2 thin strips of green bell pepper (optional)
2 small sprigs of mint (optional)

Directions

In a blender, combine the vegetable juice, lime juice, 1 celery stalk, hot pepper sauce, Worcestershire sauce, horseradish, vodka, and crushed ice. Season with salt and pepper. Cover, and blend until smooth.

Use two large frozen beer mugs, highball or pint glasses. Place one cocktail onion at the bottom of each glass. Put 1/2 cup of ice cubes into each glass. Use a vegetable peeler to pull a few strips off of the carrot for each glass. Put in a slice of green pepper. Divide the blended mixture evenly between the two glasses.

On cocktail toothpicks, place a green olive, a cocktail onion, and a lime wedge. Attach each one to a celery stalk so that when inserted, this garnish is on the top of the drink. Sprinkle on a few more carrot strips, and garnish each drink with a sprig of mint.

Party Corned Beef Puffs

Ingredients

 1/2 cups finely chopped deli
orned beef
 tablespoons chopped onion
 tablespoons Dijon mustard
 tablespoon mayonnaise
/4 teaspoon prepared
orseradish
 cup beer
/2 cup butter
 cup flour
/4 teaspoon salt
 eggs

Directions

Mix together the corned beef, onion, mustard, mayonnaise, and horseradish. Cover and refrigerate.

Preheat an oven to 450 degrees F (230 degrees C).

In a large pot, bring beer and butter to a rolling boil. Stir in flour and salt until the mixture forms a ball. Transfer the dough to a large mixing bowl. Using a wooden spoon or stand mixer, beat in the eggs one at a time, mixing well after each. Drop by teaspoonfuls onto a lightly greased baking sheet.

Bake for 10 minutes in the preheated oven. Reduce temperature to 350 degrees F (175 degrees C) and bake an additional 10 minutes until golden brown. Centers should be dry.

When the shells are cool, split the puffs and fill with the corned beef mixture. Refrigerate until ready to serve.

Bacon Wrapped Bratwurst

Ingredients

4 bratwurst
3 (12 ounce) cans light beer
5 tablespoons brown sugar
1 teaspoon cayenne pepper
6 slices bacon, cut in half

Directions

Poke bratwurst several times with a small fork, and place into a saucepan with the beer. Bring to a boil over high heat, then reduce heat to medium, and simmer for 15 minutes. Remove the bratwurst from the beer, and allow to cool to room temperature.

Preheat oven to 425 degrees F (220 degrees C). Line a baking sheet with aluminum foil, and place a wire rack on top.

Toss the brown sugar and cayenne pepper together in a large bowl and set aside. Cut each bratwurst into three pieces, wrap each piece with half strip of bacon, and secure with a toothpick. Toss the bratwurst with the cayenne mixture to coat, then place onto the prepared baking sheet.

Bake in preheated oven until the bacon is brown and crisp, 25 to 35 minutes.

Ingredients

2 cups ketchup
1 (12 fluid ounce) can or bottle beer
3/4 cup packed brown sugar
3 pork chops

Directions

Preheat oven to 350 degrees F (175 degrees C).

In a medium bowl, combine the ketchup, brown sugar and beer. Mix well and pour into a 9x13 inch baking dish. Place the pork chops over this mixture in the dish.

Bake, uncovered, at 350 degrees F (175 degrees C) for 1 hour, or internal pork temperature reaches 160 degrees F (175 degrees C). (Note: Place foil over pork chops if they start to brown too quickly.)

Beer Cheese Soup IV

Ingredients

2 cups cauliflower florets
1 tablespoon margarine
1/2 cup chopped onion
1 clove garlic, minced
1 teaspoon Worcestershire sauce
1 (12 fluid ounce) can or bottle beer
1 (14.5 ounce) can chicken broth
3 tablespoons cornstarch
3 tablespoons water
2 cups half-and-half cream
2 cups shredded Cheddar cheese

Directions

In a small saucepan over medium heat, cook cauliflower in water to cover until just tender, 5 to 10 minutes. Drain and set aside.

In a large pot over medium heat, melt margarine. Stir in onion, garlic and Worcestershire and cook until onion is translucent. Pour in beer and bring to a boil. Pour in chicken broth and return to a boil. Then reduce heat, stir in cauliflower, and heat through.

In a small bowl, combine cornstarch and 3 tablespoons water, stirring to dissolve. Set aside. Stir half-and-half and Cheddar into the soup until the cheese melts. Stir in cornstarch mixture and continue to cook and stir until soup thickens. Serve at once.

Bubba's Beer Bread

Ingredients

cups self-rising flour
tablespoons white sugar
teaspoon onion powder
teaspoon dried dill, or to taste
teaspoon salt
(12 fluid ounce) can beer, room
temperature
ounces cubed Cheddar cheese,
r to taste

Directions

Preheat the oven to 350 degrees F (175 degrees C). Lightly grease a 9 or 10 inch cast iron skillet.

In a large bowl, stir together the self-rising flour, sugar, onion powder, dill weed and salt. Pour in the beer, and stir until all of the dry is incorporated. Stir as lightly as possible so as not to deflate the beer. Fold in cheese cubes.

Bake for 45 to 60 minutes, or until the top springs back when lightly touched. The bread should rise way above the edge of the pan.

BBQ Chuck Roast

Ingredients

1 (5 pound) chuck roast
1 cup barbeque sauce
1 cup teriyaki sauce
1 (12 fluid ounce) can or bottle beer
3 teaspoons minced garlic
3 teaspoons thinly sliced fresh ginger root
1 onion, finely chopped
3 teaspoons coarsely ground black pepper
2 teaspoons salt

Directions

In a large bowl, mix barbeque sauce, teriyaki sauce, beer, garlic, ginger, onion, black pepper, and salt. Place the roast into the marinade, cover and refrigerate for six hours, turning often.

Preheat an outdoor grill for indirect heat. Remove the roast from the marinade, and pour the marinade into a saucepan. Bring to a boil, and cook for 5 minutes. Set aside for use as a basting sauce.

Thread the roast onto a rotating barbecue spit above indirect heat. Cook the roast for two hours, or until the internal temperature of the roast is at least 145 degrees F (63 degrees C). Baste often during the last hour with reserved marinade.

Smokin' Scovilles Turkey Chili

Ingredients

2 tablespoons olive oil
1 onion, chopped
5 cloves garlic, minced
2 small green bell peppers, seeded and chopped
1 habanero pepper, seeded and chopped
2 pounds lean ground turkey
2 tablespoons chili powder
2 teaspoons red pepper flakes
1 tablespoon paprika
1 tablespoon ground cumin
2 teaspoons dried oregano
1 teaspoon ground black pepper
1 (1 ounce) envelope instant hot chocolate mix
2 teaspoons seasoned salt
1 tablespoon Worcestershire sauce
1 teaspoon liquid smoke flavoring
2 (14.5 ounce) cans diced tomatoes with green chile peppers, drained
1 (8 ounce) can tomato sauce
1 (15 ounce) can kidney beans, drained
1/2 cup cheap beer
1/2 cup canned whole kernel corn
1 tablespoon hot pepper sauce

Directions

Heat the olive oil in a large saucepan over medium heat. Add the onion, garlic, green peppers and habanero pepper; cook and stir until the onion is transparent. Push these to one side of the pot, and crumble in the ground turkey. Cover, and cook for about 5 minutes, stirring occasionally, or until the meat is no longer pink. Stir everything together so the garlic doesn't burn.

Season with chili powder, red pepper flakes, paprika, cumin, oregano, pepper, hot cocoa mix and seasoned salt. Stir in Worcestershire sauce, liquid smoke, diced tomatoes with green chilies, tomato sauce and kidney beans. Crack open a beer, and pour in about 1/3. Drink or discard the rest. Partially cover the pan, and simmer over medium heat for about 50 minutes, stirring occasionally.

Mix in the corn and hot pepper sauce, and simmer for about 10 more minutes. Remove from the heat and allow to cool for a few minutes before serving.

Sweet Easter Quick Bread

Ingredients

2 (12 ounce) bottles beer
2 pounds dark brown sugar
1/2 cup butter or margarine
6 eggs
1 teaspoon vanilla extract
9 cups all-purpose flour
1/4 cup baking powder
3 cups raisins
3 cups candied mixed fruit

Directions

Preheat oven to 350 degrees F (175 degrees C). Grease 4 9x5 inch loaf pans.

In a large saucepan, combine beer, sugar and butter over medium-low heat. When the ingredients melt into each other remove from the stove top and let cool. When the mixture is cool, mix in beaten eggs and vanilla extract.

In a large bowl, combine flour, baking powder, raisins and mixed fruits. Stir beer mixture slowly into the dry mixture, incorporating and mixing as you go. Pour mixture into the prepared loaf pans.

Bake in a preheated 350 degrees F (175 degrees C) oven for 90 minutes.

Overnight Pork Roast With Cabbage

ngredients

 teaspoons caraway seeds,
rushed and divided
 cloves garlic, minced
 teaspoons salt
 teaspoon ground black pepper
 pounds boneless pork loin roast
 tablespoons olive oil, divided
 onion, thinly sliced
 carrots
 bay leaves
 1/2 pounds shredded fresh
abbage
 (12 fluid ounce) can or bottle
eer
 tablespoons molasses
 cup beef broth
 potatoes, cooked and mashed
alt and pepper to taste

Directions

In a small bowl, combine 2 teaspoons of the crushed caraway seeds, garlic, salt and ground black pepper. Rub the pork with the dry rub mixture, cover and refrigerate for 24 hours.

Preheat oven to 350 degrees F (175 degrees C).

Heat 1 tablespoon of the oil in a large skillet over medium high heat. Add the onion, carrots, bay leaves, 1 teaspoon of the crushed caraway seeds and salt and pepper to taste. Saute for 8 minutes, or until vegetables are tender. Transfer this to a 10x15 inch roasting pan.

In the same skillet over high heat, combine 1/2 tablespoon of the olive oil, half (1 1/4 pounds) of the cabbage, and 1/2 teaspoon crushed caraway seeds. Saute, stirring often, until this cooks down, about 5 to 10 minutes. Transfer this to the roasting pan and repeat with another 1/2 tablespoon of oil, the remaining half (1 1/4 pounds) of the cabbage, and the remaining crushed caraway seeds. Once cooked down, transfer this to the roasting pan.

Heat the remaining olive oil in the same skillet over medium high heat. Place the pork loin in the heated oil and brown well on all sides. Set the roast on top of all the vegetables in the roasting pan. Add the beer and molasses to the skillet and bring to a boil, scraping up all the browned bits on the bottom of the skillet. Pour this and the broth over the pork roast and vegetables. Season with salt and pepper to taste.

Bake at 350 degrees F (175 degrees C) for 45 minutes. Turn pork over and bake until the internal temperature of the pork reaches 150 degrees F (65 degrees C). At this point, remove the pan from the oven and let the pork sit on a cutting board for 5 minutes. Then slice the pork into serving size pieces. Discard the bay leaves. Return the sliced pork to the pan resting over the vegetables. Top off with the mashed potatoes.

Bake at 350 degrees F (175 degrees C) for 10 to 15 minutes, or until potatoes are lightly browned.

Three-Pepper Rice and Chicken Pot

Ingredients

1/2 pound andouille sausage links
1 poblano chile
1 red bell pepper
3 tablespoons canola oil
1 1/2 pounds skinless, boneless chicken thighs, cut into 1 1/2-inch chunks
3 tablespoons Cajun-style seasoning
1 1/2 tablespoons butter
2 yellow onions, finely chopped
2 banana (or hot) peppers, seeded and chopped
2 celery ribs, finely chopped
6 cloves garlic, minced
1 shallot, minced
3 cups long grain white rice
1 1/2 tablespoons butter
3 cups chicken stock
1 (10 ounce) can tomato sauce
1 (10 ounce) can diced tomatoes with mild green chilies, undrained
1 (12 fluid ounce) can or bottle beer
salt to taste
1 cup frozen corn kernels, thawed

Directions

Preheat your oven's broiler. Line a baking sheet with a sheet of foil.

Cook andouille sausage in a skillet over medium heat until cooked through, about 15 minutes. Remove from skillet and cut into 1/4-inch slices; set aside.

While the sausage is cooking, cut the peppers in half lengthwise and remove the stem and seeds. Place peppers, cut-side-down onto baking sheet and place into preheated oven. Broil peppers until the skins blacken, about 7 minutes, then place into a bowl and cover with plastic wrap. Allow the peppers to steam for 10 minutes until the skins loosen, then remove and discard blackened skins; chop peppers into 1/2 inch pieces and set aside.

Heat the canola oil in a stockpot over high heat. Toss the chicken with Cajun seasoning and sear in batches in the oil until light brown and no longer pink in the center, about 6 minutes. Remove chicken, leaving oil in the stockpot, and drain on paper towels.

Add 1 1/2 tablespoons of butter to the oil. Stir in the onion, banana peppers, celery, garlic, and shallot; cook until the onions are translucent, 3 to 4 minutes. Stir in rice and 1 1/2 tablespoon butter. Stir in the chicken stock, tomato sauce, and diced tomato with chilies. Cover and simmer until liquid is mostly absorbed into the rice, 10 to 12 minutes. Stir in the beer and cover; cook another 5 minutes until the rice is tender. Season with salt, then mix in the corn, poblano, bell pepper, chicken, and andouille sausage. Return to a simmer, then turn off heat and allow to rest 5 minutes before serving.

Beer Cooked Chicken

Ingredients

1 (12 fluid ounce) can or bottle beer

4 skinless, boneless chicken breast halves

2 tablespoons butter

1 cup sliced fresh mushrooms

1 tablespoon grated Parmesan cheese

Directions

To Marinate: Pour 1/2 of the beer into a nonporous glass dish or bowl. Add chicken breasts, toss to coat, cover dish and refrigerate for 30 minutes to marinate.

Melt 1 tablespoon of the butter in a large skillet over medium heat. Add mushrooms and saute for 5 to 10 minutes or until cooked; remove from skillet and reserve, keeping warm.

Melt remaining 1 tablespoon butter in skillet over medium high heat and add chicken. Saute 5 to 6 minutes each side or until cooked through and juices run clear. Reduce heat to low, pour remaining beer over chicken and add reserved mushrooms. Cover skillet and let simmer for 5 to 10 minutes. Sprinkle with cheese and serve.

Beer Cheese Dip I

Ingredients

1 (8 ounce) package cream cheese, softened
1 (8 ounce) package processed cheese food, diced
1/2 (12 fluid ounce) can beer, room temperature
1 clove garlic, peeled and crushed

Directions

In a medium bowl, whip together cream cheese, processed cheese food, beer and garlic. Continue whipping until smooth.

Terry's Beer Chicken

ngredients

- bone-in chicken breast halves, at and skin trimmed
- teaspoon garlic powder
- teaspoon chili powder
- alt and ground black pepper to aste
- onions, thinly sliced
- potatoes, thinly sliced
- tablespoons butter
- (12 fluid ounce) can or bottle eer
- /4 cup shredded Cheddar heese

Directions

Rinse and pat dry the chicken breasts. Rub the garlic powder and chili powder onto the surface of the chicken; season with salt and pepper.

Melt the butter in a large skillet over medium heat; lay the chicken into the skillet with the bone side facing down. Add the onions. Cover the skillet and cook, stirring the onions occasionally, 15 minutes. Turn the chicken and continue cooking until the chicken is no longer pink at the bone and the juices run clear, about 30 minutes. An instant-read thermometer inserted near the bone should read 165 degrees F (74 degrees C).

Add the potatoes to the skillet, return the cover to the skillet, and cook until the potatoes are cooked through, 7 to 10 minutes. Pour the beer into the skillet and allow the mixture to cook uncovered until the liquid is mostly absorbed, 7 to 10 minutes. Remove the chicken to a platter and set aside. Sprinkle the cheese over the potato and onion mixture; cook until the cheese is melted. Serve hot with the chicken breasts.

Marinated Venison

Ingredients

2 pounds venison (deer meat)
1/2 (10 fluid ounce) bottle Worcestershire sauce
1 (12 fluid ounce) can or bottle beer
1 1/2 cups all-purpose flour
1 tablespoon onion salt
1 tablespoon garlic powder
vegetable oil for frying

Directions

Pound venison flat, and cut into 1 inch strips; place in a large bowl. Pour in Worcestershire sauce and beer. Cover, and refrigerate for 1 hour or more.

In a shallow bowl, combine flour, onion salt and garlic powder. Drag soaked meat through the flour mixture. Heat oil in a large heavy skillet, and fry meat until golden brown.

Poor Man's Beer Batter Fish

Ingredients

cup beer, or as needed
(7 ounce) container shake and
pour buttermilk pancake mix
2 pounds trout fillets
1/2 cup oil for frying

Directions

Heat oil in a large skillet over medium heat.

Pour beer into the pancake mix container in place of the water it calls for. Make the batter as thick or thin as you prefer. Close the lid, give it a few shakes, and boom it's done.

Dip fish into the batter using a pair of tongs, or if you want to dirty a dish, pour the batter in a bowl first. If you cut your fish into smaller pieces, you can toss them into the container, close the lid and shake it a couple of times, then carefully remove the coated pieces.

Remove the fish from the batter using tongs, and place into the hot oil. Fry the fish until golden brown on both sides, 3 to 4 minutes per side.

Una's Cheddar Beer Bread (bread machine dough

Ingredients

1 (12 fluid ounce) can or bottle premium lager
2 tablespoons margarine
2 tablespoons milk
4 cups all-purpose flour
2 teaspoons salt
2 tablespoons sugar
4 teaspoons yeast
1 teaspoon ground black pepper
1 teaspoon ground cayenne pepper
1/2 teaspoon onion powder
1/2 teaspoon garlic powder
1/2 teaspoon dried marjoram
1/2 teaspoon dried basil
8 ounces reduced-fat extra-sharp Cheddar cheese
2 tablespoons margarine, melted

Directions

Grease two (9x5 inch) loaf pans.

In a medium saucepan over medium heat, warm beer slightly. Stir in milk and 2 tablespoons margarine to melt. Pour contents into bread machine pan. Pour in flour. Make a well in the center of the flour, and sprinkle salt onto one side of the mound that forms. Into the well, pour the sugar and yeast. Sprinkle with pepper, onion, garlic, and herbs. Begin the dough cycle.

Meanwhile, slice the cheese into pea-size crumbles. Avoid using shredded cheese, as it may clump. Once the dough forms into a sticky ball, gradually add the cheese crumbles.

As the cycle continues and the cheese fully incorporates into the dough, the ball should still be somewhat soft and sticky. If it is too dry, add a bit of milk.

When the cycle has completed, punch down the dough, and divide it in half. Place each half into a greased loaf pan, and allow the dough to rise, about 45 to 60 minutes.

Preheat the oven to 350 degrees F (175 degrees C).

When the dough has risen, bake for 1 hour, or until the loaves are golden brown and make a hollow sound when thumped. Immediately turn out onto a cooling rack, and brush with melted margarine. Cool completely before cutting.

ngredients

- pounds pork baby back ribs
- pinch black pepper
- pinch salt
- pinch crushed red pepper
- cups barbecue sauce
- (12 ounce) bottles porter beer, oom temperature

Directions

Cut ribs into small portions of 2 or 3 bones each. Bring a large pot of water to a boil. Season water a pinch each of salt, black pepper, and crushed red pepper to the water. Boil ribs in seasoned water for 20 minutes. Drain, and let the ribs sit for about a half an hour.

Meanwhile, preheat an outdoor grill for high heat.

Lightly coat the ribs with barbecue sauce. Cook the ribs over high heat for a 5 to 10 minutes on each side to get a nice grilled look to them.

Place grilled ribs in a slow cooker. Pour remaining barbecue sauce and one bottle of beer over the ribs; this should cover at least half of the ribs. Cover, and cook on High for 3 hours. Check ribs every hour or so, and add more beer if needed to dilute sauce. Stir to get the ribs on top into the sauce. The ribs are done when the meat is falling off the bone. The ribs were cooked completely in the first process, the rest is about flavor and texture.

Dubliner and GuinnessB®

Ingredients

1 (8 ounce) package cream cheese, softened
7 fluid ounces GuinnessB® Draught Beer
1/4 teaspoon Worcestershire sauce
1 clove garlic, minced
1 (8 ounce) package Dubliner Irish cheese, shredded

Directions

Place the cream cheese in the bowl of a food processor; pulse the cream cheese while adding the Guinness and Worcestershire sauce. Add the garlic and Dubliner cheese; process until smooth. Spoon the mixture into a serving bowl; cover. Chill in refrigerator overnight or 8 hours before serving.

Mexican-Style Fajitas

Ingredients

pound trimmed skirt steak
(12 ounce) bottle beer
/3 cup freshly squeezed key-lime
juice
onion, cut into rings
large green bell pepper, cut into
ings
teaspoon onion powder
teaspoon lemon pepper
seasoning
teaspoon garlic powder
teaspoon garlic salt

Directions

Stir together the beer, lime juice, onion, and bell pepper in a large glass or ceramic bowl. Pound the skirt steaks to 1/4 inch thick, and mix into the marinade. Cover the bowl with plastic wrap, and marinate in the refrigerator for 2 hours.

Preheat an outdoor grill for medium-high heat, and lightly oil the grate. Remove the skirt steak from the marinade. Discard the remaining marinade. Mix the onion powder, lemon pepper, garlic powder, and garlic salt together in a small bowl. Sprinkle the steaks with the spice mix on all sides.

Cook the steaks until they are firm, hot in the center, and well done, about 7 minutes per side. An instant-read thermometer inserted into the center should read 155 degrees F (65 degrees C).

Cajun Deep-Fried Turkey

Ingredients

2 cups butter
1/4 cup onion juice
1/4 cup garlic juice
1/4 cup Louisiana-style hot sauce
1/4 cup Worcestershire sauce
2 tablespoons ground black pepper
1 teaspoon cayenne pepper
7 fluid ounces beer
3 gallons peanut oil for frying, or as needed
1 (12 pound) whole turkey, neck and giblets removed

Directions

Melt the butter in a large saucepan over medium heat. Add the onion juice, garlic juice, hot sauce, Worcestershire sauce, black pepper, cayenne pepper and beer. Mix until well blended.

Use a marinade injecting syringe or turkey baster with an injector tip to inject the marinade all over the turkey including the legs, back, wings, thighs and breasts. Place in a large plastic bag and marinate overnight in the refrigerator. Do not use a kitchen trash bag. If your turkey is large, you can use an oven bag.

When it's time to fry, measure the amount of oil needed by lowering the turkey into the fryer and filling with enough oil to cover it. Remove the turkey and set aside.

Heat the oil to 365 degrees F (185 degrees C). When the oil has come to temperature, lower the turkey into the hot oil slowly using the hanging device that comes with turkey deep-fryers. The turkey should be completely submerged in the oil. Cook for 36 minutes, or 3 minutes per pound of turkey. The turkey is done when the temperature in the thickest part of the thigh reaches 180 degrees F (80 degrees C). Turn off the flame and slowly remove from the oil, making sure all of the oil drains out of the cavity. Allow to rest on a serving platter for about 20 minutes before carving.

Barb's Guinness®-n-Cabbage Delight

Ingredients

tablespoon toasted pumpkin seed oil

medium shallots, diced

teaspoons minced fresh ginger root

cups shredded red cabbage

cups shredded napa cabbage

cup Irish stout beer (e.g., Guinness)

/4 teaspoon salt

/4 teaspoon freshly ground black pepper

Directions

Heat the pumpkin seed oil in a skillet over medium-high heat. Place shallots and ginger in the skillet, and cook until tender. Mix in red cabbage and napa cabbage, and cook about 2 minutes. Pour in the beer. Season with salt and pepper. Reduce heat to medium, cover skillet, and continue cooking 5 minutes, or until cabbage is tender.

Blackjack Brisket

Ingredients

10 pounds untrimmed beef brisket
1 (12 fluid ounce) can beer (optional)
1 large onion, quartered
2 cloves garlic, minced
1 tablespoon salt
1 tablespoon pepper
2 (18 ounce) bottles hickory smoke flavored barbeque sauce
1 cup blackstrap molasses
2 tablespoons liquid smoke flavoring

Directions

Preheat the oven to 250 degrees F (120 degrees C).

Place brisket in a large roasting pan (disposable aluminum foil pan is fine). Pour beer over the meat, and place onion sections on top. Season with garlic, salt and pepper. Combine the barbeque sauce, molasses and liquid smoke; pour over the roast. Cover pan with aluminum foil.

Place pan on the center rack of the preheated oven, and bake for 6 to 8 hours, or until beef is fork tender. Remove from the oven and let stand for about 10 minutes before slicing across the grain into 1/8 inch slices.

Melissa's Mussels

Ingredients

5 pounds mussels, cleaned and debearded
1 large onion, diced
1 (14.5 ounce) can diced tomatoes
5 large cloves garlic, chopped
1 (12 fluid ounce) can or bottle beer
1/2 cup red wine
2 tablespoons peppercorns in brine, crushed (optional)

Directions

In a large pot (or the kitchen sink basin), soak the mussels 10 minutes in enough lightly salted cold water to cover.

In a separate large pot, mix the onion, tomatoes, garlic, beer, wine, and peppercorns. Place the mussels in the pot, and bring to a boil. Cook 10 minutes, reduce heat to low, and continue cooking 5 minutes, until mussels open. Discard unopened mussels.

Beer Cheese Soup VII

Ingredients

3/8 cup butter
1 1/2 cups chopped onion
3 (12 fluid ounce) cans or bottles beer
1 1/2 cups diced carrots
3 stalks celery, diced
1 tablespoon ground cumin
2 1/2 teaspoons salt
3/4 teaspoon ground nutmeg
1/8 teaspoon ground cloves
1/4 teaspoon ground black pepper
3 cups sour cream
12 ounces processed cheese, cubed

Directions

In a large pot over medium heat, melt butter. Cook onion in butter until tender. Stir in beer, carrots and celery. Bring to a boil, then reduce heat, cover and simmer 10 minutes.

Stir in cumin, salt, nutmeg, cloves and pepper. Bring to a boil again, then reduce heat, cover and simmer 30 minutes.

Remove from heat and stir in sour cream and cheese. Serve at once.

Garlic Chicken Marinara

Ingredients

2 (8 ounce) packages angel hair
pasta
6 skinless, boneless chicken
breast halves, cut into bite size
pieces
2 tablespoons olive oil
1 medium head garlic, minced
4 cups stewed tomatoes
1 large onion, chopped
2 cups fresh sliced mushrooms
4 large tomatoes, diced
1/2 red bell pepper, diced
1/2 green bell pepper, diced
1 1/2 cups corn
1/2 cup light beer

Directions

In a large skillet pan fry the boneless skinless chicken breasts in the olive oil and half of the head of minced garlic. Cook chicken until the juices run clear.

In a large saucepan bring stewed tomatoes, the other half of the garlic, onion, mushrooms, fresh tomatoes, red and green bell pepper, corn and beer to a boil. When sauce is boiling, add the cooked chicken and simmer for 1 hour.

In a large pot cook with boiling salted water cook angel hair pasta until al dente. Drain.

Toss pasta with garlic chicken sauce. Serve warm.

El Rancho Beer Dip

Ingredients

2 (8 ounce) packages cream cheese, softened
1 (8 ounce) container sour cream
3/4 cup beer
1 (1 ounce) package dry Ranch-style dressing mix

Directions

Place the softened cream cheese, sour cream, beer, and Ranch dressing mix in a blender. Blend until well mixed for 2 to 3 minutes, scraping down the sides of the container as needed. Pour into a bowl and cover. Refrigerate for at least 1 hour before serving.

Beer Dip I

Ingredients

2 (8 ounce) packages cream cheese, softened
1 (1 ounce) package ranch dressing mix
2 cups shredded Cheddar cheese
1/3 cup beer

Directions

In a medium bowl, combine cream cheese and dressing mix. Stir in Cheddar cheese, and then beer. The mixture will appear mushy. Cover bowl, and refrigerate for at least 3 hours, overnight if possible.

Tomato Curry Chicken

Ingredients

4 skinless, boneless chicken breast halves
2 tablespoons butter
1 onion, chopped
2/3 cup beer
1 (10.75 ounce) can condensed tomato soup
1 teaspoon curry powder
1/2 teaspoon dried basil
1/2 teaspoon ground black pepper
1/4 cup grated Parmesan cheese

Directions

Preheat oven to 350 degrees F (175 degrees C).

Place chicken in a 9x13 inch baking dish. Melt butter in a medium skillet over medium heat. Saute onion, then stir in beer, soup, curry powder, basil and pepper. Reduce heat to low and simmer for about 10 minutes, then pour over chicken.

Bake at 350 degrees F (175 degrees C) for 1 hour; sprinkle with cheese for last 10 minutes of baking.

Savory Cheese Soup

Ingredients

3 (14.5 ounce) cans chicken broth
 small onion, chopped
 large carrot, chopped
 celery rib, chopped
/4 cup chopped sweet red
pepper
2 tablespoons butter or margarine
 teaspoon salt
/2 teaspoon pepper 1/3
cup all-purpose flour 1/3
cup cold water
 (8 ounce) package cream
cheese, cubed and softened
2 cups shredded Cheddar cheese
 (12 fluid ounce) can beer
(optional)
Optional toppings: croutons,
popcorn, cooked crumbled
bacon, sliced green onions

Directions

In a slow cooker, combine the first eight ingredients. Cover and cook on low for 7-8 hours.

Combine flour and water until smooth; stir into soup. Cover and cook on high 30 minutes longer or until soup is thickened.

Stir in cream cheese and cheddar cheese until blended. Stir in beer if desired. Cover and cook on low until heated through. Serve with desired toppings.

Gourmet Root Beer Float

Ingredients

1/2 pint vanilla ice cream
1 (12 fluid ounce) can or bottle root beer
1/2 cup whipped cream
4 maraschino cherries

Directions

Place 1 scoop of ice cream into each of two tall glasses. Pour root beer carefully over the ice cream. Add another scoop and repeat. If possible, repeat again.

Pete's Tailgate Turkey Marinade

Ingredients

1 tablespoon Worcestershire sauce
1 tablespoon crab boil seasoning
1/4 cup orange juice
1/2 cup honey
1/4 cup olive oil
1 cup beer
1 1/2 teaspoons salt
2 tablespoons Creole seasoning
2 cloves garlic

Directions

In the container of a blender, combine the Worcestershire sauce, crab boil, orange juice, honey, olive oil, beer, salt, Creole seasoning, and garlic. Cover and puree until smooth. Make sure there are no large pieces of garlic to clog the syringe. Store in a sealed container or plastic bag overnight in the refrigerator.

Rickyrootbeer

Ingredients

1/2 fluid ounce vanilla vodka
1/2 fluid ounce Irish cream liqueur
4 fluid ounces root beer

Directions

Pour the vodka and Irish cream into a shot glass. Pour the root beer into a tumbler. Drop the entire shot glass into the root beer and drink immediately.

Brisket With Gravy

Ingredients

(4 pound) fresh beef brisket*
1/2 teaspoon pepper
1 large onion, thinly sliced, separated into rings
1 (12 ounce) can beer or nonalcoholic beer
1/2 cup chili sauce
3 tablespoons brown sugar
2 garlic cloves, minced
2 tablespoons cornstarch
1/4 cup cold water

Directions

Place beef in a roasting pan. Sprinkle with pepper and top with onion. Combine the beer, chili sauce, brown sugar and garlic; stir until sugar is dissolved. Pour over meat. Cover and bake at 325 degrees F for 3-1/2 hours. Uncover; bake 15-30 minutes longer or until onions are lightly browned and meat is tender. Remove meat and onions to a serving platter and keep warm.

Pour drippings and loosened browned bits into a saucepan. Skim fat. Combine cornstarch and water until smooth. Gradually stir into pan drippings. Bring to a boil; cook and stir for 2 minutes or until thickened. Slice meat thinly across the grain. Serve with gravy.

Bread Machine Pizza Dough

Ingredients

1 cup flat beer
2 tablespoons butter
2 tablespoons sugar
1 teaspoon salt
2 1/2 cups all-purpose flour
2 1/4 teaspoons yeast

Directions

Put beer, butter, sugar, salt, flour, and yeast in a bread machine in the order recommended by the manufacturer. Select Dough setting, and press Start.

Remove dough from bread machine when cycle is complete. Roll or press dough to cover a prepared pizza pan. Brush lightly with olive oil. Cover and let stand 15 minutes.

Preheat oven to 400 degrees F (200 degrees C).

Spread sauce and toppings on top of dough. Bake until crust is lightly brown and crispy on the outside, about 24 minutes.

Queso Catfish

Ingredients

4 (6 ounce) fillets catfish
1/4 cup lime juice
1/2 cup cheap beer
1/4 cup yellow cornmeal
1 cup finely crushed tortilla chips
1/2 teaspoon salt
1/4 teaspoon cayenne pepper
2 tablespoons lime juice
2 tablespoons canola oil
4 ounces processed cheese, cubed
1 teaspoon chili powder
1 teaspoon ground cumin
1/2 chipotle pepper, minced
2 tablespoons chopped fresh cilantro (optional)

Directions

In a shallow dish, stir together 1/4 cup of lime juice and beer. Place fish in the dish, and turn to coat. Marinate for 30 minutes.

Preheat the oven to 400 degrees F (200 degrees C). Coat a roasting rack with cooking spray, and place over a baking sheet.

Rinse fish with cold water, and pat dry. Discard the marinade. In one dish, stir together the cornmeal, tortilla chip crumbs, salt and pepper. In another dish, stir together 2 tablespoons of lime juice and canola oil. Dip fillets into the lime and oil, then into the cornmeal mixture to coat. Place the fish onto the roasting rack.

Bake fish for 8 to 10 minutes, or until it flakes easily with a fork. While the fish is baking, combine the processed cheese, chili powder, cumin, and chipotle pepper in a small saucepan over medium-low heat. Cook and stir until melted and smooth.

Place fish onto serving plates, and spoon the cheese sauce over them. Top with a sprinkling of cilantro leaves, if desired.

Schweinshaxe

Ingredients

1 carrot, diced
1 onion, peeled and diced
1 leek, chopped
1 stalk celery, diced
2 meaty pork knuckles
2 tablespoons vegetable shortening
1 teaspoon whole black peppercorns
salt to taste
1/4 cup beer
1 pinch ground cumin, or to taste

Directions

Place the carrot, onion, leek, celery, and pork knuckles into a large stockpot. Throw in the peppercorns, and season with salt to taste. Add enough water to the pot to cover the vegetables. Cover, and cook over medium heat for 2 to 3 hours, or until everything is tender. Remove the knuckles from the water, and drain. Reserve vegetables and cooking liquid.

Preheat the oven to 425 degrees F (220 degrees C). Melt the shortening in an enamel coated cast iron baking dish or pan. Place the drained pork knuckles, cooked vegetables, and about 2 cups of the cooking liquid into the pan.

Bake for 30 minutes in the preheated oven. During the last 10 minutes, sprinkle with beer in which a good amount of salt has been dissolved. Dust lightly with cumin to increase flavor. Serve with potato or white bread dumplings, or sauerkraut salad. In Bavaria, the cooking liquid and juices are strained, and served as an accompanying sauce.

Ingredients

2 (12 fluid ounce) bottles dark
beer (such as Negra Modelo®)
1 lime
6 chicken drumsticks
coarse salt to taste

Directions

Preheat the oven's broiler and set the oven rack about 8 inches from the heat source.

Pour the beer into a deep, broiler-safe baking pan. Cut half of the lime into thin slices and place into the beer. Squeeze the other half of the lime into the beer, and place the chicken legs on top. Sprinkle with coarse salt to taste.

Broil for 15 minutes, then turn the legs over, and continue broiling until the chicken is no longer pink at the bone and the juices run clear, about 15 minutes more. An instant-read thermometer inserted near the bone should read at least 165 degrees F (74 degrees C).

Beer Cheese Dip II

Ingredients

2 (8 ounce) packages cream cheese, softened
2 (8 ounce) packages shredded Cheddar cheese
1/2 teaspoon garlic powder
1/2 cup beer
1 (1 pound) loaf round bread

Directions

Place cream cheese, Cheddar cheese, garlic powder and beer in a large bowl. Using an electric mixer, blend until smooth.

Remove and reserve top of round bread. Hollow out the loaf, reserving removed bread pieces.

Spoon cream cheese mixture into the hollowed loaf. Replace bread top between servings. Use the reserved removed bread pieces for dipping.

Easy Beer and Ketchup Meatballs

Ingredients

1 (28 ounce) bottle ketchup
24 fluid ounces beer
1 1/2 pounds ground beef
2 teaspoons garlic powder
1 onion, chopped

Directions

Preheat oven to 400 degrees F (200 degrees C).

Place the beer and ketchup in a slow cooker on high setting and allow to simmer..

Meanwhile, in a large bowl, combine the ground beef, garlic powder and onion, mixing well. Form mixture into meatballs about 3/4 inch in diameter. Place meatballs in a 9x13 inch baking dish.

Bake at 400 degrees F (200 degrees C) for 20 minutes.

Transfer meatballs to the slow cooker with the beer and ketchup and simmer for 3 hours; sauce will thicken.

Wisconsin Slow Cooker Brats

Ingredients

8 bratwurst
2 (12 fluid ounce) cans or bottles beer
1 onion, sliced
3/4 cup ketchup

Directions

Place bratwurst, beer, onion, and ketchup in a slow cooker. Pour water over mixture until everything is covered. Set slow cooker to HIGH and cook for 4 hours.

Preheat an outdoor grill for high heat and lightly oil grate.

Grill bratwurst on preheated grill until they are browned, about 5 minutes.

Kahlua Root Beer Float

Ingredients

1/2 fluid ounces Kahlua 3/4
uid ounce vanilla vodka
plash of orange juice
scoop vanilla ice cream
Root beer

Directions

Shake the Kahlua, vodka, and orange juice in a cocktail shaker with ice, strain into an ice-filled highball glass or soda glass, add the ice cream, and top with root beer.

BBQ Beer Brat Kabobs

Ingredients

1 (19 ounce) package Bob EvansB® Beer Bratwurst, cut into 1-inch pieces
1 green bell pepper, cut into 1-inch pieces
1 medium zucchini, cut into 1-inch pieces
1 red bell pepper, cut into 1-inch pieces
1 medium yellow squash, cut into 1-inch pieces
2 cups fresh button mushroom caps
1 medium red onion, cut into 1-inch pieces
2 cups Bob EvansB® Wildfire BBQ Sauce
6 (10 inch) wooden skewers

Directions

Soak wooden skewers in water 30 minutes. Alternately thread bratwurst and vegetables onto skewers. Grill or broil kabobs 12 to 15 minutes or until brats are cooked through, turning and brushing occasionally with barbecue sauce. Refrigerate leftovers.

Belgium Beef Stew

Ingredients

2 pounds beef stew meat, cut into
1 inch cubes
3/8 cup all-purpose flour
1/4 cup butter
4 onions, diced
1 2/3 cups water
1 sprig fresh thyme
2 bay leaves
salt and ground black pepper to
taste
1 (12 fluid ounce) can or bottle
brown beer
1 slice bread
1 tablespoon prepared mustard
2 carrots, cut into 1 inch pieces
1 tablespoon white wine vinegar
2 tablespoons brown sugar

Directions

Dredge the meat in the flour. In a Dutch oven, melt the butter over medium heat. Brown meat in butter, then add the onions and fry until glazed. Stir in water and vinegar. Season with thyme, bay leaves, and salt and pepper to taste. Cover, and simmer for 30 minutes.

Mix in the beer. Spread mustard over bread, then add the bread and the carrots to the meat. Cover, and simmer for 30 minutes. Mix in the brown sugar (two tablespoons is a minimum! A lot of people prefer more).

Sausage 'n Stout Cheese Soup

Ingredients

4 potatoes, peeled and diced
6 cups water
2 (12 fluid ounce) bottles cream stout beer
2 pounds kielbasa sausage, sliced thin
4 green onions, diced
2 teaspoons salt
1/2 teaspoon ground black pepper
1/4 teaspoon liquid smoke flavoring
1/2 teaspoon cayenne pepper
1/2 teaspoon dried mustard powder
1 pound shredded Cheddar cheese
2 cups milk

Directions

Bring potatoes, water, and beer to a boil in a large saucepan over high heat. Reduce heat to medium-low, cover, and simmer 5 minutes. Stir in the sausage, green onions, salt, black pepper, cayenne pepper, mustard powder, and liquid smoke. Cover and simmer until the potatoes are completely tender, about 15 minutes.

When the potatoes are tender, stir in the Cheddar cheese until completely melted, then add the milk. Heat through, stirring until cheese has melted but do not boil.

Sesame Tempura Green Beans

Ingredients

2 quarts oil for deep frying
1 cup all-purpose flour
1/4 cup sesame seeds
1 (12 fluid ounce) can or bottle beer
3/4 pound fresh green beans, rinsed and trimmed
salt to taste
3 tablespoons soy sauce
3 teaspoons lime juice
1 teaspoon white sugar

Directions

Heat oil in deep-fryer to 375 degrees F (190 degrees C).

In a medium bowl, mix the flour, sesame seeds and beer until smooth. Roll the beans in the flour mixture to coat.

Deep fry the coated beans in small batches until golden brown, about 1 1/2 minutes per batch. Drain on paper towels. Salt to taste.

In a small bowl, whisk together the soy sauce, lime juice and sugar to use as a dipping sauce.

Easy Beer Bread Mix

Ingredients

2 1/2 cups self-rising flour
1/2 cup all-purpose flour
1/4 cup brown sugar
1 teaspoon baking powder
1/2 teaspoon salt
1/2 teaspoon onion powder
3/4 teaspoon Italian seasoning
1 (12 fluid ounce) can beer
1/4 cup butter or margarine, melted

Directions

Preheat oven to 375 degrees F (190 degrees C). Lightly grease a 9x5 inch baking pan.

In a bowl, mix the self-rising flour, all-purpose flour, brown sugar, baking powder, salt, onion powder, and Italian seasoning. Pour in the beer, and mix just until moistened. Transfer to the prepared baking pan. Top with the melted butter.

Bake 45 to 55 minutes in the preheated oven, until a toothpick inserted in the center comes out clean. Cool on a wire rack.

Strip and Go Naked

Ingredients

30 (12 fluid ounce) cans or bottles
Keystone Light beer
1 3/4 liters vodka
2 (12 ounce) cans frozen
lemonade concentrate, thawed

Directions

In a 4 to 5 gallon sports drink dispenser, combine the light beer, vodka and lemonade concentrate. Stir gently to disperse the lemonade. Put the lid on and serve.

Beer Chops II

Ingredients

1 onion, chopped
2 pork chops butterfly cut
1 (12 fluid ounce) can or bottle beer
2 cubes chicken bouillon

Directions

Arrange chopped onions in bottom of slow cooker. Lay butterfly chops on top, separating if you wish. Pour in beer and drop in chicken bouillon cubes. Cook on low for 6 to 8 hours.

Bronco Burger

Ingredients

5 fresh jalapeno peppers
4 pounds ground beef
salt and pepper to taste
1 egg
1/4 cup steak sauce, (e.g. Heinz 57)
1/4 cup minced white onion
1 teaspoon hot pepper sauce (e.g. Tabascoв„ў)
1 pinch dried oregano
1 tablespoon Worcestershire sauce
1 teaspoon garlic salt
1/4 cup crushed FritosB® corn chips
8 large potato hamburger buns
8 slices pepperjack cheese

Directions

Preheat a grill for high heat. When the grill is hot, roast the jalapeno peppers until blackened on all sides. Place in a plastic bag to sweat and loosen the blackened skin. Rub the skin off, then seed if desired, and chop.

In a large bowl, use your hands to mix together the chopped jalapenos, ground beef, salt, pepper, egg, steak sauce, onion, hot pepper sauce, oregano, Worcestershire sauce, garlic salt and FritosB®. Divide into 8 balls, and flatten into patties.

Grill patties for 10 to 15 minutes, turning once, or until well done. I always drink one beer, then flip, drink another beer, then remove from the grill and place on buns. Top each one with a slice of pepperjack cheese and pig out!

Red Pepper Chicken

Ingredients

1 cup water
1/2 cup uncooked long grain white rice
1 tablespoon extra virgin olive oil
4 fluid ounces Mexican beer
2 boneless, skinless chicken breast halves
2 tablespoons chili powder
1 tablespoon dried oregano
salt and pepper to taste
1/2 red bell pepper, chopped
1 fresh red chile pepper, finely chopped
1/2 clove garlic, minced
1/2 lime, thinly sliced
1/2 lemon, thinly sliced
1/4 cup grated Romano cheese

Directions

In a saucepan, bring the water and rice to a boil. Cover, reduce heat, and simmer 25 minutes, until rice is tender.

Heat the olive oil and 1 fluid ounce beer in a skillet over medium heat. Place the chicken in the skillet, and season with chili powder, oregano, salt, and pepper. Mix in the remaining beer, red bell pepper, chile pepper, garlic, lime, and lemon. Cook about 15 minutes, until the chicken is no longer pink and juices run clear.

Place the chicken and vegetables over the cooked rice, and sprinkle with Romano cheese to serve.

Michilada

Ingredients

coarse salt
3 cubes ice
1 lime, juiced
1 (12 fluid ounce) can or bottle
Mexican beer
1/2 teaspoon steak sauce
1 dash cayenne pepper
1 dash black pepper
1 pinch dried oregano
1 pinch dried basil

Directions

Moisten the rim of a large beer glass, then press it into salt. Place a few ice cubes in bottom of glass, followed by the lime juice. Pour in half of the beer, then season with steak sauce, cayenne pepper, black pepper, oregano and basil. Slowly pour in the remaining beer. Stir.

Beer Margarita

Ingredients

1 (6 ounce) can frozen lemonade concentrate
8 fluid ounces vodka
3 (12 fluid ounce) cans or bottles beer

Directions

Empty lemonade concentrate into pitcher (do not add water!). Pour in vodka and beer. Serve over ice.

Tanya's Jamaican Spice Bread

Ingredients

Batter:
3 1/4 cups all-purpose flour
4 teaspoons baking powder
2 teaspoons ground cinnamon
1 teaspoon ground nutmeg
1/2 teaspoon ground allspice
1 pinch salt
1 egg
1 cup milk
1/3 cup beer (such as Heineken®)
1 3/4 cups brown sugar
1/2 cup melted butter
1 teaspoon browning sauce
1 teaspoon vanilla extract
1 teaspoon lime juice
1 cup raisins

Glaze:
1/2 cup brown sugar
1/2 cup water

Directions

Preheat an oven to 325 degrees F (165 degrees C). Grease two 8x4-inch loaf pans.

Whisk the flour, baking powder, cinnamon, nutmeg, allspice, and salt together in a bowl; set aside. Beat the egg in a mixing bowl; whisk in the milk, beer, and 1 3/4 cups of brown sugar until the brown sugar has dissolved. Stir in the butter, browning sauce, vanilla extract, and lime juice until blended. Add the flour mixture and raisins. Stir until no dry lumps remain. Pour the batter into the prepared loaf pans.

Bake in the preheated oven until a toothpick inserted into the center comes out clean, about 1 hour.

When the bread is nearly finished, combine 1/2 cup brown sugar and the water in a small saucepan. Bring to a boil over high heat and boil until the sugar is thick and syrupy, about 5 minutes. Pour the glaze over the bread once it's done; return the bread to the oven and bake 5 minutes longer. Cool in the pans for 5 minutes before turning out onto a wire rack to cool completely.

Moroccan Inspired Apricot-Braised Chicken

Ingredients

1 tablespoon olive oil
4 chicken thighs
1 large onion, halved lengthwise and cut into thick slices
1 tablespoon minced garlic
1/2 cup unsulfured apricots, halved
1/2 teaspoon ground ginger
1/2 teaspoon ground cumin
1/2 teaspoon ground allspice
1 cup beer (preferably lager)
salt and pepper to taste

Directions

Heat olive oil in a deep skillet over medium-high heat. Brown chicken thighs on both sides until golden, about 3 minutes per side. Set chicken aside, then stir in onion and garlic; cook for 1 to 2 minutes until the onion has softened. Stir in apricots and season with ginger, cumin, and allspice. Cook for 1 minute until spices are fragrant.

Pour beer into pan, scraping the bottom of the pan to dissolve the browned bits. Add chicken, cover, and reduce heat to medium-low. Simmer gently until the chicken begins to fall away from the bone, about 30 minutes.

Amber Beer Cheese Dip

Ingredients

2 (10 ounce) packages extra-sharp Cheddar cheese (such as Cracker Barrel®), shredded
3 tablespoons minced garlic
1 (12 ounce) bottle amber beer
1/4 teaspoon cayenne pepper, or to taste

Directions

Place the shredded cheese and garlic in the bowl of a food processor. With food processor running, slowly pour in the beer, scraping sides of the bowl as necessary; process until evenly blended. Season with cayenne pepper to taste. Transfer to a serving bowl, cover, and chill until ready to serve.

Beer Cheese Soup II

Ingredients

1 tablespoon margarine
1/2 cup chopped onion
1/2 teaspoon minced garlic
1 teaspoon Worcestershire sauce
1 (12 fluid ounce) can or bottle light beer
1 (14.5 ounce) can chicken broth
3 tablespoons cornstarch
2 cups half-and-half
2 cups shredded sharp Cheddar cheese

Directions

Melt the butter or margarine in a 4 1/2 quart soup pot over medium heat. Add the onion, garlic and Worcestershire sauce and stir well. Add the beer and raise the heat to high and boil for 3 minutes to evaporate the alcohol. Add the chicken broth and bring the soup back to a boil. Lower the heat to medium-low and simmer.

Combine the cornstarch with 3 tablespoons water and stir until smooth. Set aside.

Add the half-and-half and shredded cheese to the soup. Stir constantly until the cheese melts. Then stir in the cornstarch mixture. Stir constantly until the soup is thick, about 2 minutes. Serve garnished with bacon bits.

Ingredients

1 (2 to 3 pound) whole chicken, cut into pieces
1 tablespoon olive oil
2 onions, chopped
3 cloves garlic, crushed
1/2 green bell pepper, chopped
1/2 (15 ounce) can tomato sauce
1 pinch saffron
salt to taste
2 cubes chicken bouillon
1 1/2 cups uncooked white rice
1 cup beer
1 (15 ounce) can peas, drained
1/2 red bell pepper, roasted and sliced

Directions

Heat oil in a large skillet over medium high heat. Saute chicken until lightly browned; remove from skillet and set aside.

Saute onion, garlic and green bell pepper until soft; stir in tomato sauce, saffron, salt and bouillon and return chicken pieces to skillet. Cook for 10 minutes, then add rice and reduce heat to low.

Add beer and simmer for 8 to 10 minutes, stirring occasionally, until rice is tender. Finally, stir in peas with liquid and garnish with roasted red bell pepper.

Vickie's Beer Bread

Ingredients

3 cups self-rising flour
3 tablespoons white sugar
1 (12 fluid ounce) can or bottle
beer, room temperature
1/4 cup margarine, melted

Directions

Preheat oven to 375 degrees F (190 degrees C). Lightly grease a 9x5 inch baking pan.

In a large bowl, combine flour, sugar and beer. Mix just until blended. Scoop into prepared baking pan. Pour melted margarine on top of loaf.

Bake in preheated oven for 45 to 60 minutes, until bottom of loaf sounds hollow when tapped.

Beer Butt Chicken

Ingredients

1 cup butter
2 tablespoons garlic salt
2 tablespoons paprika
salt and pepper to taste
1 (12 fluid ounce) can beer
1 (4 pound) whole chicken

Directions

Preheat an outdoor grill for low heat.

In a small skillet, melt 1/2 cup butter. Mix in 1 tablespoon garlic salt, 1 tablespoon paprika, salt, and pepper.

Discard 1/2 the beer, leaving the remainder in the can. Add remaining butter, garlic salt, paprika, and desired amount of salt and pepper to beer can. Place can on a disposable baking sheet. Set chicken on can, inserting can into the cavity of the chicken. Baste chicken with the melted, seasoned butter.

Place baking sheet with beer and chicken on the prepared grill. Cook over low heat for about 3 hours, or until internal temperature of chicken reaches 180 degrees F (80 degrees C).

Pizza Sauce and Dough

Ingredients

PIZZA DOUGH:
1/4 cup warm water (100 to 110 degrees)
1 teaspoon active dry yeast
1 teaspoon white sugar
4 cups bread flour
2 tablespoons Italian-style seasoning
1 teaspoon salt, divided
1 1/4 cups flat beer
1 tablespoon olive oil

PIZZA SAUCE:
2 tablespoons olive oil
1/3 cup chopped onion
2 tablespoons chopped garlic
1 (28 ounce) can roma tomatoes, with juice
2 (6 ounce) cans tomato paste
1 tablespoon chopped fresh basil
1 tablespoon chopped fresh parsley
1 teaspoon chopped fresh oregano
1/2 teaspoon black pepper

Directions

In a small bowl, dissolve yeast and sugar in warm water. Let stand until creamy, about 10 minutes.

In a food processor, combine flour, Italian seasoning and salt. Pulse until mixed. Add yeast mixture, flat beer and oil. Pulse until a ball is formed. Scrape dough out onto a lightly floured surface, and knead for several minutes until dough is smooth and elastic. Allow dough to rest for 2 to 3 minutes. Divide dough in half, and shape into balls. Place dough balls in separate bowls, and cover with plastic wrap. Allow to rise at room temperature for about 1 hour, then store in the refrigerate overnight.

To make the sauce: Heat olive oil in a saucepan over medium heat. Saute onions until tender. Stir in garlic, and cook for 1 minute. Crush tomatoes into saucepan. Add tomato paste, basil, parsley and oregano. Simmer for 10 minutes.

Ingredients

1 cup butter, sliced
2 teaspoons minced garlic
1/4 cup lemon pepper
1/4 cup salt-free spicy seasoning
blend
5 pounds potatoes, cubed
1 green bell pepper, chopped
1 yellow bell pepper, chopped
1 orange bell pepper, chopped
1 sweet onion, chopped
3 (12 fluid ounce) cans beer
16 ounces shredded Mexican-
style cheese blend

Directions

Preheat an outdoor grill for medium heat.

Line the bottom of a 9x13 inch foil roasting pan with half of the butter, garlic, lemon pepper, and salt-free spicy seasoning blend. Place half of the potatoes, green bell pepper, yellow bell pepper, orange bell pepper and onion in the roasting pan and cover with the remaining butter, garlic, lemon pepper, and seasoning blend. Mix in the remaining potatoes, green bell pepper, yellow bell pepper, orange bell pepper and onion. Pour in the beer until it reaches just below the top layer of vegetables.

Cover pan with foil, place pan on the grill grate, and cook 1 1/2 hours, or until the potatoes are tender. Remove pan from the grill, cover with the shredded cheese, and let stand until the cheese has melted.

Country Margaritas

Ingredients

2 (12 fluid ounce) cans frozen
lemonade concentrate
1 1/2 cups vodka
2 (12 fluid ounce) cans beer
ice cubes

Directions

In a large jug or pitcher, mix together the lemonade concentrate,
vodka and beer. Stir, and serve over ice.

Football Sunday Beer Cheese Soup

Ingredients

2 tablespoons butter
2 tablespoons minced onion
1 teaspoon minced garlic
1 1/2 tablespoons Worcestershire sauce
1 (12 fluid ounce) can or bottle light beer
1 3/4 cups chicken broth
1 teaspoon ground mustard
2 cups half-and-half cream
3 cups shredded Cheddar cheese
1/4 cup flour
1/4 cup cornstarch
1/4 cup water
salt and pepper to taste

Directions

Melt the butter in a saucepan over medium heat; cook the onion and garlic in the butter until the onion is tender, about 5 minutes. Pour in the Worcestershire sauce and beer; bring to a boil for 3 to 5 minutes. Stir the chicken broth and mustard. Reduce heat to medium-low and pour in the half-and-half while stirring.

Toss together the shredded Cheddar cheese and flour in a bowl; add to the liquid mixture in small batches until melted.

Whisk together the cornstarch and warm water in a small bowl; stir into the cheese mixture; season with salt and pepper. Heat and stir until thick; serve hot.

Joe's Famous Michelada

Ingredients

coarse salt for rim of mug, or as needed
ice cubes
1/4 teaspoon salt
1 lemon, juiced
1 dash hot pepper sauce (such as Tabasco®), or to taste
1/2 teaspoon soy sauce
1 1/2 cups tomato and clam juice cocktail (such as Clamato®), or as needed
1/2 cup cold beer

Directions

Dip the rim of a chilled 1-pint mug or schooner into coarse salt, and fill the mug with ice cubes. Add 1/4 teaspoon of salt, lemon juice, hot pepper sauce, and soy sauce. Pour in the tomato and clam juice cocktail, top up the mug with beer, and stir gently. As you drink, you can keep topping up your mug with more beer.

Western Style Beef Jerky

Ingredients

3/4 cup beer
3/4 cup teriyaki sauce
1/2 cup Worcestershire sauce
1/3 cup soy sauce
1/3 cup water
3 tablespoons liquid smoke
1 1/2 teaspoons ketchup
1 teaspoon red pepper flakes
1 1/2 teaspoons salt
1/2 teaspoon onion salt 1/4
easpoon cracked black
pepper, or to taste
1/4 teaspoon garlic powder
1 pound beef round steak

Directions

Stir together beer, teriyaki sauce, Worcestershire sauce, soy sauce, water, liquid smoke, and ketchup in a large bowl. Stir in red pepper flakes, salt, onion salt, pepper, and garlic powder until blended.

Cut the round steak into long strips about 1 inch wide by 1/4 inch thick. Toss the meat with the marinade until the strips are well coated. Tightly cover the bowl, and marinate in the refrigerator at least 6 hours.

Prepare jerky in a food dehydrator according to manufacturer's directions.

Mexican Mole Poblano Inspired Chili

Ingredients

2 tablespoons olive oil
1 1/2 cups chopped onions
1 cup chopped green pepper (optional)
1 (4 ounce) can chopped green chilies (optional)
8 large garlic cloves, chopped
3 pounds cubed beef stew meat
5 tablespoons chili powder
2 tablespoons ground cumin
2 teaspoons dried basil
1 teaspoon cayenne pepper
1 teaspoon crushed red pepper flakes
1 teaspoon dried oregano
1 teaspoon dried thyme
1 bay leaf
1 cinnamon stick
1 (28 ounce) can crushed tomatoes in puree
1 (14.5 ounce) can beef broth
1 (12 fluid ounce) bottle dark beer
1 (6 ounce) can tomato paste
1 (15 ounce) can chili beans
2 (1 ounce) squares bittersweet chocolate, chopped
salt and pepper, to taste

Directions

Heat oil in a large, heavy pot over medium-high heat. Stir in onions, green peppers, green chilies, and garlic. Cook and stir until onions are soft and translucent, about 8 minutes. Add the stew meat to the pot, cook until well browned, about 5 minutes.

Stir the chili power, cumin, basil, cayenne pepper, crushed red pepper, oregano, thyme, bay leaf, and cinnamon stick into the pot. Cook and stir until spices are aromatic, about 2 minutes.

Pour the crushed tomatoes, beef broth, and beer into the pot; stir in the tomato paste. Bring chili to a simmer and cook until beef is very tender and the liquids have thickened, about 1 hour and 15 minutes.

Mix the chili beans and chocolate into the chili. Simmer until the chocolate has melted and the chili is hot, 5 minutes. Remove cinnamon stick and bay leaf. Season to taste with salt and pepper.

Beer Chops I

Ingredients

1 onion, sliced
2 pork chops butterfly cut
1 (12 fluid ounce) can or bottle
beer
2 cubes chicken bouillon

Directions

Arrange onion slices on bottom of slow-cooker. Cut butterfly chops in half and place on top of onions. Pour in beer and add chicken bouillon cubes. Cover and cook and low 6 to 8 hours.

Beer Beef Stew II

Ingredients

2 tablespoons vegetable oil
3 1/2 pounds beef stew meat, cut into 1 1/2 inch pieces
1 cup all-purpose flour
2 large potatoes, chopped
1 cup chopped carrots
3/4 cup chopped celery
3/4 cup chopped onion
3 cloves garlic, chopped
1 tablespoon dried basil
1 tablespoon dried thyme
1 cup chili sauce
1 cup beer
1/4 cup brown sugar

Directions

Heat the oil in a skillet over medium heat. Place the beef stew meat and flour in a large resealable plastic bag, and shake to coat. Transfer coated meat to the skillet, and cook about 1 minute, until browned.

Mix the potatoes, carrots, celery, onion, and garlic in a slow cooker. Place browned beef over the vegetables, and season with basil and thyme.

In a bowl, mix the chili sauce, beer, and brown sugar, and pour over meat in the slow cooker.

Cover slow cooker, and cook 8 hours on Low or 2 hours on High.

Drunken Winter Stew

Ingredients

3 potatoes, peeled and cubed
1/4 cup chopped onion
1/2 medium head cabbage, sliced
1 (15 ounce) can kidney beans, drained and rinsed
3 cups water
1 (12 fluid ounce) can beer
1 tablespoon prepared Dijon-style mustard
1/4 tablespoon garlic powder
ground black pepper to taste
salt to taste

Directions

Bring potatoes, onions, and water to a boil, lower heat to simmer.

Add cabbage and mustard. Slowly add about 1/2 the beer (it will foam up a bit). Cover loosely. Let simmer 15 minutes, stirring occasionally.

Add the beans, spices, and more/all of the beer to taste. Remove lid, let simmer another 10 minutes or until potatoes are tender. Add water if necessary. Re-spice if needed before serving.

Vegetarian Tourtiere

Ingredients

2 cups vegetable broth
2 cups texturized vegetable protein (TVP)
1/2 cup dried vegetable flakes
3 tablespoons butter
1 cup onion, minced
2 cups mushrooms, minced
2 cups bread crumbs
1 teaspoon freshly cracked peppercorns
1/2 teaspoon sea salt
1/2 teaspoon dried thyme leaves
1/2 teaspoon dried summer savory leaves
1 pinch ground cloves
1 pinch fresh ground nutmeg
1 (12 fluid ounce) bottle beer, room temperature
1 egg, beaten
1 tablespoon milk
2 (9 inch) refrigerated pie crusts
1 teaspoon water

Directions

Pour the vegetable broth into a saucepan and bring to a boil over high heat. Measure the texturized vegetable protein and vegetable flakes into a large mixing bowl. Pour the boiling broth over the texturized vegetable protein and vegetable flakes; soak for 15 minutes.

Meanwhile, melt the butter in a large skillet over medium-high heat, add the mushrooms and onions; cook and stir until soft, about 10 minutes.

Stir the texturized vegetable protein and vegetable flake mixture in with the mushroom and onions. Pour the beer into the skillet with the vegetable mixture; remove from heat and cool.

Preheat oven to 450 degrees F (230 degrees C).

Whisk the egg and milk together in a small bowl.

Line a deep dish pie plate with one round of the prepared pastry. Pour the vegetable mixture into the pastry shell. Prepare the top pastry by cutting a 2 to 3-inch hole in the center of the round using a knife or a decorative cookie cutter.

Moisten the edges of the bottom round with water. Place the top round of prepared pastry on top of the meat filling, pressing around the edges and crimping to seal. Brush the top of the pastry with the egg and milk mixture.

Bake in the preheated 450 degree F (230 degrees C) oven for 15 minutes. Lower the oven temperature to 375 degrees F (190 degrees C) and continue baking until the crust is golden brown, 30 to 40 minutes.

Czech Roast Pork

Ingredients

2 tablespoons vegetable oil
1 tablespoon prepared mustard
2 tablespoons caraway seeds
1 tablespoon garlic powder
1 tablespoon salt
2 teaspoons ground black pepper
5 pounds pork shoulder blade roast
3 medium onions, chopped
1/2 cup beer
1 tablespoon cornstarch
2 tablespoons butter

Directions

In a bowl, form a paste using the vegetable oil, mustard, caraway seeds, garlic powder, salt, and pepper. Rub over the pork roast, and let sit about 30 minutes.

Preheat oven to 350 degrees F (175 degrees C).

Arrange the onions in the bottom of a large roasting pan. Pour in the beer. Place the roast, fat side down, on top of the onions. Cover the pan with foil.

Roast 1 hour in the preheated oven. Remove foil, turn roast, and score the fat. Continue roasting 2 1/2 hours, or to a minimum internal temperature of 160 degrees F (70 degrees C). Remove from heat, reserving pan juices, and let sit about 20 minutes before slicing thinly.

In a saucepan, bring the reserved pan juices to a boil. Mix in the butter and cornstarch to thicken, reduce heat, and simmer 5 to 10 minutes. Serve with the sliced pork.

JoeDogg's Spicy Red Beer

Ingredients

1 (12 fluid ounce) can or bottle beer
1 (5.5 ounce) can tomato-vegetable juice cocktail
1 dash Louisiana-style hot sauce
1 dash Worcestershire sauce
1 pinch seasoning salt

Directions

In a frozen beer mug combine tomato-vegetable juice, hot sauce, Worcestershire sauce and seasoning salt. Pour in cold beer.

Steamed Blue Crabs

Ingredients

36 live blue crabs
1/2 cup seafood seasoning (such as Old Bay®)
1/2 cup salt
3 cups beer
3 cups distilled white vinegar
1/4 cup seafood seasoning (such as Old Bay®)

Directions

Right before cooking, carefully place each crab upside down and stick a knife through the shell, just behind mouth.

Combine 1/2 cup seafood seasoning, salt, beer, and vinegar in a large stockpot over high heat. Bring to a strong simmer.

Fit a screen over the beer mixture and layer the crabs on the screen. Be sure that the crabs are above the simmering liquid. Cover.

Steam crabs until they turn bright orange and all of the blue/green color is gone, 20 to 30 minutes. Sprinkle with the remaining 1/4 cup seafood seasoning before serving.

Irish Stew, My Way

Ingredients

2 tablespoons olive oil
1 small sweet onion, diced
1/4 teaspoon salt
1/2 teaspoon freshly ground black pepper
1 tablespoon dried Italian seasoning
3 cloves garlic, crushed
1 pound cubed lamb stew meat
1 pound cubed pork stew meat
1 (14.5 ounce) can beef broth
3 carrots, cut into 1/2 inch pieces
1 medium turnip, quartered and cut into 1/2 inch pieces
2 parsnips, peeled and cut into 1/2 inch pieces
1 red bell pepper, seeded and cut into 1 inch pieces
1 yellow bell pepper, seeded and cut into 1 inch pieces
1 green bell pepper, seeded and cut into 1 inch pieces
1 medium sweet onion, cut into large chunks
2 stalks celery, cut into 1/2 inch pieces
1 (12 fluid ounce) can beer
8 small red potatoes, quartered
2 tablespoons cornstarch

Directions

Heat olive oil in a large skillet over medium heat. Place 1 onion in skillet, and season with salt, pepper, and Italian seasoning. Mix in garlic. Cook and stir until tender. Mix in the lamb and pork, and cook until evenly brown. Reduce heat to low, and pour in beef broth. Simmer 30 minutes.

Transfer the skillet mixture to a large pot. Mix in the carrots, turnip, parsnips, red bell pepper, yellow bell pepper, green bell pepper, remaining onion, and celery. Pour in the beer. Cover, and cook 2 hours over low heat.

Remove 1/2 cup stew liquid. Stir potatoes into pot, and continue cooking 30 minutes, or until potatoes are tender. About 15 minutes before serving, mix cornstarch into the reserved liquid. Stir into the stew to thicken.

Flip Flop Grilled Chicken

Ingredients

3/4 cup butter
2 (12 fluid ounce) cans or bottles beer
1 tablespoon steak seasoning
1 1/2 teaspoons seasoning salt
1 dash black pepper
8 boneless, skinless chicken breast halves
3 medium green bell peppers, thinly sliced

Directions

Preheat an outdoor grill for high heat.

Melt the butter in a saucepan over medium heat. Mix in the beer, steak seasoning, seasoning salt, and black pepper. Coat the chicken with this mixture.

Lightly oil the grill grate. Arrange chicken breasts on the grill. Cook for about 20 minutes, brushing frequently with the beer mixture during the last 10 minutes, until chicken is no longer pink and juices run clear. Discard any remaining beer mixture. Top chicken with green bell pepper slices to serve.

Cheese Dip with Beer

Ingredients

1 (1 pound) loaf round pumpernikel rye bread
1 (8 ounce) package shredded Cheddar cheese
1 (8 ounce) package shredded mozzarella cheese
1 (8 ounce) package cream cheese, softened
1 cup beer
1 teaspoon garlic salt

Directions

Cut a large hole in the top of the loaf of bread to form a bowl; set onto a serving platter.

Melt the cream cheese in a large saucepan over medium heat; stir in the Cheddar cheese, mozzarella cheese, beer, and garlic salt; heat, stirring continually, until all the cheese is melted; pour the hot cheese mixture into the bread bowl.

Wonderful Fried Fish Tacos

Ingredients

1 cup dark beer
1 cup all-purpose flour
1/2 teaspoon salt
1 1/2 pounds cod fillets, cubed
1 quart vegetable oil for frying
20 (6 inch) corn tortillas
5 cups shredded cabbage
1 cup mayonnaise
1/4 cup salsa
1 lime, cut into wedges

Directions

In a shallow bowl, whisk together beer, flour, and salt.

Rinse fish, and pat dry. Cut into 10 equal pieces.

In a large saucepan, heat 1 inch oil to 360 degrees F (168 degrees C). Using a fork, coat fish pieces in batter. Slide coated fish into hot oil in batches; adjust heat to maintain oil temperature. Fry until golden, about 2 minutes. Lift out with a slotted spoon, and drain briefly on paper towels; keep warm. Repeat to fry remaining fish.

Stack 2 tortillas. Place a piece of fish and 1/2 cup cabbage in the center of the tortillas. Garnish with mayonnaise, lime wedges and salsa

Lobster Tails Steamed in Beer

Ingredients

2 whole lobster tail
1/2 (12 fluid ounce) can beer

Directions

In a medium saucepan, over medium to high heat, bring the beer to a boil.

If lobster tails are still in the shell, split the shell lenghtwise first.

Place a steamer basket on top of the saucepan. place thawed lobster tails in basket and cover. Reduce heat and simmer for 8 minutes.

Cheddar Beer Triangles

Ingredients

2 cups baking mix
1/2 cup shredded Cheddar
cheese
1/2 cup beer

Directions

Preheat an oven to 450 degrees F (230 degrees C). Grease a baking sheet.

Stir the baking mix, Cheddar cheese, and beer in a bowl until the mixture clings together. Knead briefly on a lightly-floured surface until the dough just holds together. Pat the dough into a 6-inch circle and cut into 10 wedges; place the wedges onto the prepared baking sheet.

Bake in the preheated oven until browned on the bottom and golden brown on top, 8 to 10 minutes.

Bone-In Ham Cooked in Beer

Ingredients

20 pounds bone-in ham
1 (20 ounce) can sliced pineapple
2 (12 fluid ounce) cans beer

Directions

Preheat oven to 325 degrees F (165 degrees C). Grease an 18 quart roasting pan.

Place the ham, with the fattier side up, in the roaster. Use toothpicks to secure pineapple rings on the ham. Pour the beer over the ham. Place lid on roasting pan.

Bake 6 to 8 hours, or until cooked through.

Remove the pineapple rings and let sit 15 minutes before slicing.

German-Style Beer Brat Sandwich

Ingredients

2 pretzel rolls, split
2 Hillshire Farm® Miller High
Life™ Beer Brats
3 tablespoons Dijon mustard
2 cups thinly sliced (1/8 inch)
yellow onions
1 tablespoon olive oil
1/2 tablespoon whole grain
mustard
1/4 teaspoon black pepper
Kosher salt

Directions

While grilling Hillshire Farm Miller High Life Beer Brats, baste with Dijon mustard.

In a small saute pan heat olive oil over medium heat. Add onions and cook until soft and golden brown, approximately 15 minutes.

Stir whole grain mustard into onions and season to taste with salt and pepper.

Place one grilled brat in pretzel roll and generously top with caramelized onions.

Baked Pretzels

Ingredients

1 cup beer
1 tablespoon margarine
2 tablespoons white sugar
1 teaspoon salt
3 cups all-purpose flour
3/4 teaspoon active dry yeast
1 egg
1 tablespoon warm water (110 degrees F/45 degrees C)
2 tablespoons kosher salt

Directions

Measure first 6 ingredients in order listed into baking pan. Select: Dough/Pasta Setting and press start.

When the cycle is complete remove dough to a lightly floured surface. If necessary, knead in enough flour to make dough easy to handle. Roll into a 14X9 inch rectangle. With a sharp knife, cut into eighteen 14X1/2 inch strips. Gently pull each strip into a rope 16 inches long. To shape into pretzels: Curve ends of each rope to make a circle; cross ends at top. Twist ends once and lay over bottom of circle. Place on greased baking sheets. DO NOT LET RISE.

Combine lightly beaten egg and 1tablespoon water; brush on pretzels. Sprinkle with kosher salt. Bake in a preheated 350 degrees F (175 degrees C) oven for 18-20 minutes or until done. Remove from sheets and let pretzels cool on wire rack. Enjoy!

Tex-Mex Patty Melts

Ingredients

1 pound ground beef
3 tablespoons chili seasoning mix
2 chipotle peppers in adobo sauce, minced
1/2 fluid ounce beer
1/4 cup mayonnaise
1 chipotle pepper in adobo sauce, minced
6 (1 ounce) slices white bread
6 (1/2 ounce) slices pepperjack cheese

Directions

Mix together the ground beef, chili seasoning mix, 2 minced chipotle peppers with adobo sauce, and the beer in a bowl. Divide the mixture evenly into three patties.

Stir together the mayonnaise and 1 minced chipotle pepper with adobo sauce in a small bowl. Divide the mixture between the bread slices and spread evenly. Place a slice of pepperjack cheese on top of the mayonnaise mixture on each slice of bread.

Heat a large skillet over medium-high heat. Cook the patties in the skillet until no longer pink in the center, 5 to 7 minutes each side for well done. Remove each burger to a slice of bread, sandwiching them with the remaining slices.

Drain the skillet, reserving 2 tablespoons of the grease. Heat the reserved grease in the skillet over medium-high heat. Grill the sandwiches in the skillet until the bread is golden brown and the cheese is melted, 1 to 2 minutes per side.

Cheesy Leek Strata

Ingredients

1 (1 pound) loaf sourdough bread, cut into 1/2-inch cubes
2 small leeks, white portion only, chopped
1 medium sweet red pepper, chopped
1 1/2 cups shredded Swiss cheese, divided
1 1/2 cups shredded Cheddar cheese, divided
8 eggs
2 cups milk
1/2 cup beer
2 garlic cloves, minced
1/4 teaspoon salt
1/4 teaspoon pepper

Directions

In a 13-in. x 9-in. x 2-in. baking dish coated with nonstick cooking spray, layer half of the bread cubes, half of the leeks and half of the red pepper, 3/4 cup Swiss cheese and 3/4 cup cheddar cheese. Repeat layers once.

In a bowl, whisk the eggs, milk, beer, garlic, salt and pepper. Pour over cheese. Cover with plastic wrap. Weigh strata down with a slightly smaller baking dish. Refrigerate for at least 2 hours or overnight.

Remove strata from the refrigerator 30 minutes before baking. Bake, uncovered, at 350 degrees F for 40-45 minutes or until center is set and a thermometer reads 160 degrees F. Let stand for 5-10 minutes before cutting.

Zippy Burgers

Ingredients

1/4 cup beer or beef broth
2 tablespoons Worcestershire sauce
2 teaspoons chili powder
1 teaspoon onion powder
1/2 teaspoon crushed red pepper flakes
1/4 teaspoon salt
1/4 teaspoon pepper
1 pound lean ground beef
4 hamburger buns, split

Directions

In a bowl, combine the first seven ingredients. Crumble beef over mixture and mix well. Shape into four patties.

If grilling the hamburgers, coat grill rack with nonstick cooking spray before starting the grill. Grill hamburgers, covered, over medium heat or broil 4 in. from the heat for 6-8 minutes on each side or until a meat thermometer reads 160 degrees F. Serve on buns.

Tipsy Chicken

Ingredients

6 cups water
2 cups beer
1/8 cup salt
1 teaspoon garlic powder
1 teaspoon onion powder
1 (3 pound) whole chicken
hickory or mesquite wood chips
2 tablespoons ground cumin
2 tablespoons curry powder
2 tablespoons chili powder, divided
1 tablespoon pepper
1 teaspoon salt
1/2 teaspoon paprika
1/2 teaspoon cayenne pepper

Directions

Combine brine ingredients - water, beer, 1/8 cup salt, garlic powder, and onion powder - in a large container, one that is large enough to hold the brine and the chicken. Soak whole chicken in brine for 1 hour.

Soak wood chips in water for 1 hour.

Preheat grill for indirect cooking method. Place wood chips over coals when ready to cook.

In a small bowl, combine cumin, curry, chili powder, pepper, 1 teaspoon salt, paprika, and cayenne pepper. Rub chicken inside and out with spice mixture.

Place chicken on grill, breast side down. Close lid, and cook for 30 minutes. Turn over, and cook for an additional 25 minutes, or until juices run clear and temperature is 185 degrees in the thickest part of the chicken. Keep the lid closed while cooking for even cooking, and to get more of that smoky flavor.

CPSIA information can be obtained
at www.ICGtesting.com
Printed in the USA
BVHW052153030521
606339BV00014B/2068